Riding for Ladi

by W. A. Ker

PREFACE.

This work should be taken as following on, and in conjunction with, its predecessor on "Riding." In that publication will be found various chapters on Action, The Aids, Bits and Bitting, Leaping, Vice, and on other cognate subjects which, without undue repetition, cannot be reintroduced here. These subjects are of importance to and should be studied by all, of either sex, who aim at perfection in the accomplishment of Equitation, and who seek to control and manage the saddle-horse.

W. A. K.

CONTENTS.

RIDING FOR LADIES.

CHAPTER I.

INTRODUCTORY.

What I have said on the excellence of horse-exercise for boys and men, applies equally to girls and women, if, indeed, it does not recommend itself more especially in the case of the latter. For the most part the pursuits of women are so quiet and sedentary that the body is rarely called into that complete activity of all the muscles which is essential to their perfect development, and which produces the strength and freedom of movement so indispensable to perfect grace of carriage.

The woman who has been early accustomed to horse-exercise gains a courage and nerve which it would be difficult to acquire in a more pleasant and healthful manner. She also gains morally in learning to feel a sympathy with the noble animal to whom she is indebted for so much enjoyment, and whose strength and endurance are too often cruelly abused by man. Numerous instances have occurred in my experience of the singular influence obtained by ladies over their horses by simple kindness, and I am tempted to introduce here an account of what gentle treatment can effect with the Arab. The lady who told the tale did not lay claim to being a first-rate horsewoman. Her veracity was undoubted, for her whole life was that of a ministering angel. She wrote thus: "I had a horse provided for me of rare beauty and grace, but a perfect Bucephalus in her way. She was only two generations removed from a splendid Arabian, given by the good old king to the Duke of Kent when H.R.H. went out in command to Nova Scotia. The creature was not three years old, and to all appearance unbroken. Her manners were those of a kid rather than of a horse; she was of a lovely dappled gray, with mane and tail of silver, the latter almost sweeping the ground; and in her frolicsome gambols she turned it over her back like a Newfoundland dog. Her slow step was a bound, her swift motion unlike that of any other animal I ever rode, so fleet, so smooth, so unruffled. I know nothing to which I can compare it. Well, I made this lovely creature so fond of me by constant petting, to which, I suppose, her Arab character made her peculiarly sensitive, that my voice had equal power over her, as over my faithful docile dog. No other person could in the slightest degree control her. Our corps, the 73rd Batt. of the 60th Rifles, was composed wholly of the elite of Napoleon's soldiers, taken in the

Peninsula, and preferring the British service to a prison. They were, principally, conscripts, and many were evidently of a higher class in society than those usually found in the ranks. Among them were several Chasseurs and Polish Lancers, very fine equestrians, and as my husband had a field-officer's command on detachment, and allowances, our horses were well looked after. His groom was a Chasseur, mine a Pole, but neither could ride "Fairy" unless she happened to be in a very gracious mood. Lord Dalhousie's English coachman afterwards tried his hand at taming her, but all in vain. In an easy quiet manner she either sent her rider over her head or, by a laughable manoeuvre, sitting down like a dog on her haunches, slipped him off the other way. Her drollery made the poor men so fond of her that she was rarely chastised, and such a wilful, intractable wild Arab it would be hard to find. Upon her I was daily mounted. Inexperienced in riding, untaught, unassisted, and wholly unable to lay any check upon so powerful an animal, with an awkward country saddle, which, by some fatality, was never well fixed, bit and bridle to match, and the mare's natural fire increased by high feed, behold me bound for the wildest paths in the wildest regions of that wild country. But you must explore the roads about Annapolis, and the romantic spot called the "General's Bridge," to imagine either the enjoyment or the perils of my happiest hour. Reckless to the last degree of desperation, I threw myself entirely on the fond attachment of the noble creature; and when I saw her measuring with her eye some rugged fence or wild chasm, such as it was her common sport to leap over in her play, the soft word of remonstrance that checked her was uttered more from regard to her safety than my own. The least whisper, a pat on the neck, or a stroke down the beautiful face that she used to throw up towards mine, would control her; and never for a moment did she endanger me. This was little short of a daily miracle, when we consider the nature of the country, her character, and my unskilfulness. It can only be accounted for on the ground of that wondrous power which, having willed me to work for a time in the vineyard of the Lord, rendered me immortal till the work should be done. Rather, I should say, in the words of Cooper, which I have ventured to slightly vary--

"'Tis plain the creature whom He chose to invest With queen-ship and dominion o'er the rest, Received her nobler nature, and was made Fit for the power in which she stands arrayed."

Strongly as I advocate early tuition, if a girl has not mounted a horse up to her thirteenth year, my advice is to postpone the attempt, unless thoroughly strong, for a couple of years at least. I cannot here enter the reason why, but it is good and sufficient. Weakly girls of all ages, especially those who are growing rapidly, are apt to suffer from pain in the spine. "The Invigorator" corset I have recommended under the head of "Ladies' Costume" will, to some extent, counteract this physical weakness; but the only certain cures are either total cessation from horse exercise, or the adoption of the cross, or Duchess de Berri, seat--in plain words, to ride ala cavaliere astride in a man's saddle. In spite of preconceived prejudices, I think that if ladies will kindly peruse my short chapter on this common sense method, they will come to the conclusion that Anne of Luxembourg, who introduced the side-saddle, did not confer an unmixed benefit on the subjects of Richard the Second, and that riding astride is no more indelicate than the modern short habit in the hunting field. We are too apt to prostrate ourselves before the Juggernaut of fashion, and to hug our own conservative ideas.

Though the present straight-seat side-saddle, as manufactured by Messrs. Champion and Wilton, modifies, if it does not actually do away with, any fear of curvature of the spine; still, it is of importance that girls should be taught to ride on the off-side as well as the near, and, if possible, on the cross-saddle also. Undoubtedly, a growing girl, whose figure and pliant limbs may, like a sapling, be trained in almost any direction, does, by always being seated in one direction, contract a tendency to hang over to one side or the other, and acquire a stiff, crooked, or ungainly seat. Perfect ease and squareness are only to be acquired, during tuition and after dismissal from school, by riding one day on the near and the next on the off-side. This change will ease the horse, and, by bringing opposite sets of muscles into play, will impart strength to the rider and keep the shoulders level. Whichever side the rider sits, the reins are held, mainly, in the left hand--the left hand is known as the "bridle-hand." Attempts have frequently been made to build a saddle with two flaps and movable third pommel, but the result has been far from satisfactory. A glance at a side-saddle tree will at once demonstrate the difficulty the saddler has to meet, add to this a heavy and ungainly appearance. The only way in which the shift can be obtained is by having two saddles.

CHAPTER II.

THE LADY'S HORSE.

There is no more difficult animal to find on the face of the earth than a perfect lady's horse. It is not every one that can indulge in the luxury of a two-hundred-and-fifty to three-hundred-guinea hack, and yet looks, action, and manners will always command that figure, and more. Some people say, what can carry a man can carry a woman. What says Mrs. Power O'Donoghue to this: "A heavy horse is never in any way suitable to a lady. It looks amiss. The trot is invariably laboured, and if the animal should chance to fall, he gives his rider what we know in the hunting-field as 'a mighty crusher.' It is indeed, a rare thing to meet a perfect 'lady's horse.' In all my wide experience I have met but two. Breeding is necessary for stability and speed--two things most essential to a hunter; but good light action is, for a roadster, positively indispensable, and a horse who does not possess it is a burden to his rider, and is, moreover, exceedingly unsafe, as he is apt to stumble at every rut and stone."

Barry Cornwall must have had something akin to perfection in his mind's eye when penning the following lines:--

"Full of fire, and full of bone, All his line of fathers known; Fine his nose, his nostrils thin, But blown abroad by the pride within! His mane a stormy river flowing, And his eyes like embers glowing In the darkness of the night, And his pace as swift as light. Look, around his straining throat Grace and shifting beauty float! Sinewy strength is in his reins, And the red blood gallops through his veins."

How often do we hear it remarked of a neat blood-looking nag, "Yes, very pretty and blood-like, but there's nothing of him; only fit to carry a woman." No greater mistake can be made, for if we consider the matter in all its bearings, we shall see that the lady should be rather over than under mounted.

The average weight of English ladies is said to be nine stone; to that must be added another stone for saddle and bridle (I don't know if the habit and other habiliments be included in the nine stone), and we must give them another stone in hand; or eleven stone in all. A blood, or at furthest, two crosses of blood on a good foundation, horse will carry this weight as well as it can be carried. It is a fault among thoroughbreds that they do not bend the knee sufficiently; but there are exceptions to this rule. I know of two Stud Book sires, by Lowlander, that can trot against the highest stepping hackney or roadster in the kingdom, and, if trained, could put the dust in the eyes of nine out of ten of the much-vaunted standard American trotters. Their bold, elegant, and elastic paces come up to the ideal poetry of action, carrying themselves majestically, all their movements like clockwork, for truth and regularity. The award of a first prize as a hunter sire to one of these horses establishes his claim to symmetry, but, being full sixteen hands and built on weight-carrying lines, he is just one or two inches too tall for carrying any equestrienne short of a daughter of Anak.

Though too often faulty in formation of shoulders, thoroughbreds, as their name implies, are generally full of quality and, under good treatment, generous horses. I do not chime in with those who maintain that a horse can do no wrong, but do assert that he comes into the world poisoned by a considerably less dose of original sin than we, who hold dominion over him, are cursed with.

Two-year-olds that have been tried and found lacking that keen edge of speed so necessary in these degenerate days of "sprinting," many of them cast in "beauty's mould," are turned out of training and are to be picked up at very reasonable prices. Never having known a bit more severe than that of the colt-breaker and the snaffle, the bars of their mouths are not yet callous, and being rescued from the clutches of the riding lads of the training-stable, before they are spoiled as to temper, they may, in many instances, under good tuition, be converted into admirable ladies' horses--hacks or hunters. They would not be saleable till four years old, but seven shillings a week would give them a run at grass and a couple of feeds of oats till such time as they be thoroughly taken in hand, conditioned, and taught their business. The margin for profit on well bought animals of this description, and their selling price as perfect lady's horses, are very considerable.

In my opinion no horse can be too good or too perfectly trained for a lady. Some Amazons can ride anything, play cricket, polo, golf, lawn-tennis, fence, scale the Alps, etc., and I have known one or two go tiger-shooting. But all are not manly women, despite fashion, trending in that unnatural, unlovable direction. One of their own sex describes them as "gentle, kindly, and cowardly." That all are not heroines, I admit, but no one who witnessed or even read of their devoted courage during the dark days of the Indian mutiny, can question their ability to face terrible danger with superlative valour. The heroism of Mrs. Grimwood at Manipur is fresh in our memory. What the majority are wanting in is nerve. I have seen a few women go to hounds as well and as straight as the ordinary run of first-flight men. That I do not consider the lady's seat less secure than that of the cross-seated sterner sex, may be inferred from the sketch of the rough-rider in my companion volume for masculine readers, demonstrating "the last resource," and giving practical exemplification of the proverb, "He that can quietly endure overcometh." What women lack, in dealing with an awkward, badly broken, unruly horse, is muscular force, dogged determination, and the ability to struggle and persevere. Good nerve and good temper are essentials.

Having given Barry Cornwall's poetic ideal of a horse, I now venture on a further rhyming sketch of what may fairly be termed "a good sort":--

"With intelligent head, lean, and deep at the jowl, Shoulder sloping well back, with a skin like a mole, Round-barrelled, broad-loined, and a tail carried free, Long and muscular arms, short and flat from the knee, Great thighs full of power, hocks both broad and low down, With fetlocks elastic, feet sound and well grown; A horse like unto this, with blood dam and blood sire, To Park or for field may to honours aspire; It's the sort I'm in want of--do you know such a thing? 'Tis the mount for a sportswoman, and fit for a queen!"

My unhesitating advice to ladies is Never buy for yourself. Having described what you want to some well-known judge who is acquainted with your style of riding, and who knows the kind of animal most likely to suit your temperament, tell him to go to a certain price, and, if he be a gentleman you will not be disappointed. You won't get perfection, for that never existed outside the garden of Eden, but you will be well carried and get your money's worth. Ladies are not fit to cope with dealers, unless the latter be top-sawyers of the trade, have a character to lose, and can be trusted. There has been a certain moral obliquity attached to dealing in horses ever since, and probably before, they of the House of Togarmah traded in Tyrian fairs with horses, horsemen, and mules. Should your friend after all his trouble purchase something that does not to the full realize your fondest expectation, take the will for the deed, and bear in mind "oft expectation fails, and most oft there where most it promises."

With nineteen ladies out of every score, the looks of a horse are a matter of paramount importance: he must be "a pretty creature, with beautiful deer-like legs, and a lovely head." Their inclinations lead them to admire what is beautiful in preference to what is true of build, useful, and safe. If a lady flattered me with a commission to buy her a horse, having decided upon the colour, I should look out for something after this pattern: one that would prove an invaluable hack, and mayhap carry her safely and well across country.

Height fifteen two, or fifteen three at the outside; age between six and eight, as thoroughbred as Eclipse or nearly so. The courage of the lion yet gentle withal. Ears medium size, well set on, alert; the erect and quick "pricking" motion indicates activity and spirit. I would not reject a horse, if otherwise coming up to the mark, for a somewhat large ear or for one slightly inclined to be lopped, for in blood this is a pretty certain indication of the Melbourne strain, one to which we are much indebted. The characteristics of the Melbournes are, for the most part, desirable ones: docility, good temper, vigorous constitution, plenty of size, with unusually large bone, soundness of joints and abundance of muscle. But these racial peculiarities are recommendations for the coverside rather than for the Park. The eye moderately prominent, soft, expressive, "the eye of a listening deer." The ears and the eyes are the interpreters of disposition. Forehead broad and flat. A "dish face," that is, slightly concave or indented, is a heir-loom from the desert, and belongs to Nejd. The jaws deep, wide apart, with plenty of space for the wind-pipe when the head is reined in to the chest. Nostrils long, wide, and elastic, exhibiting a healthy pink membrane. We hear a good deal of large, old-fashioned heads, and see a good many of the fiddle and Roman-nosed type, but, in my opinion, these cumbersome heads, unless very thin and fleshless, are indicative of plebeian blood.

The setting on of the head is a very important point. The game-cock throttle is the right formation, giving elasticity and the power to bend in obedience to the rider's hand. What the dealers term a fine topped horse, generally one with exuberance of carcase and light of limbs, is by no means "the sealed pattern" for a lady; on the contrary, the neck should be light, finely arched-- that peculiarly graceful curve imported from the East,--growing into shoulders not conspicuous for too high withers. "Long riding shoulders" is an expression in almost every horseman's mouth, but very high and large-shouldered animals are apt to ride heavy in hand and to be high actioned. Well-laid-back shoulders, rather low, fine at the points, not set too far apart, and well-muscled will be found to give pace with easy action.

He should stand low on the legs, which means depth of fore-rib, so essential in securing the lady's saddle, as well as ensuring the power and endurance to sustain and carry the rider's weight in its proper place. Fore-legs set well forward, with long, muscular arms, and room to place the flat of the hand between the elbows and the ribs. The chest can hardly be too deep, but it can be too wide, or have too great breadth between the fore-legs. The back only long enough to find room for the saddle is the rule, though, in case of a lady's horse, a trifle more length unaccompanied by the faintest sign of weakness, will do no harm. For speed, a horse must have length somewhere, and I prefer to see it below, between the point of the elbow and the stifle joint. Ormonde, "the horse of the century," was nearly a square, i.e. the height from the top of the wither to the ground almost equalled the length of his body from the point of the shoulder to the extremity of the buttock. Horses with short backs and short bodies are generally buck-leapers, and difficult to sit on when fencing. The couplings or loins cannot be too strong or the ribs too well sprung; the back ribs well hooped. This formation is a sign of a good constitution. The quarters must needs be full, high set on, with straight crupper, well rounded muscular buttocks, a clean channel, with big stifles and thighs to carry them. Knees and hocks clean, broad, and large, back sinews and ligaments standing well away from the bone, flat and hard as bands of steel; short well-defined smooth cannons; pasterns nicely sloped, neither too long nor too short, but full of spring; medium sized feet, hard as the nether millstone. If possible, I should select one endowed with the characteristic spring of the Arab's tail from the crupper. Such a horse would, in the words of Kingsley, possess "the beauty of Theseus, light but massive, and light, not in spite of its masses, but on account of the perfect disposition of them."

There is no need for the judge to run the rule, or the tape either, over the horse. His practised eye, almost in a glance, will take in the general contour of the animal; it will tell him whether the various salient and important points balance, and will instantly detect any serious flaw. When selecting for a lady who, he knows, will appreciate sterling worth rather than mere beauty, he may feel disposed to gloss over a certain decidedness of points and dispense with a trifle of the comely shapeliness of truthfully moulded form. Having satisfied myself that the framework is all right, I would order the horse to be sauntered away from me with a loose rein, and, still with his head at perfect liberty, walked back again. I would then see him smartly trotted backwards and forwards. Satisfied with his natural dismounted action, I should require to see him ridden in all his paces, and might be disposed to get into the saddle myself. Having acquitted himself to my satisfaction, he would then have to exhibit himself in the Park or in a field, ridden in the hands of some proficient lady-rider. A few turns under her pilotage would suffice to decide his claims to be what I am looking for. If he came up to my ideas of action, or nearly so, I should not hesitate--subject to veterinary certificate of soundness--to purchase. Finally, the gentleman to examine the horse as to his soundness would be one of my own selection. Certain of the London dealers insist upon examinations being made by their own "Vets," and "there's a method in their madness." When such a stipulation is made, I invariably play the return match by insisting upon having the certificate of the Royal College of Veterinary Surgeons, where the investigation is complete and rigorous. The very name of "the College" is gall and wormwood to many of these "gentlemen concerned about horses."

CHAPTER III.

PRACTICAL HINTS.

HOW TO MOUNT.

Previous to mounting, the lady should make a practice of critically looking the horse over, in order to satisfy herself that he is properly saddled and bridled. Particular attention should be paid to the girthing. Though ladies are not supposed to girth their own horses, occasion may arise, in the Colonies especially, when they may be called upon to perform that office. Information on this essential and too oft-neglected point may not be out of place. Odd as it may sound, few grooms know how to girth a horse properly, and to explain myself I must, for a few lines, quit the side-saddle for the cross-saddle. Men often wonder how it is that, on mounting, the near stirrup is almost invariably a hole or more the longer of the two. The reason is this: the groom places the saddle right in the centre of the horse's back and then proceeds to tighten the girths from the near or left side. The tension on the girth-holder, all from one side, cants the saddle over to the left, to which it is still further drawn by the weight of the rider in mounting and the strain put upon it by the act of springing into the saddle. This list to port can easily be obviated by the groom placing the heel of his left hand against the near side of the pommel, guiding the first or under-girth with the right hand till the girth-holder passes through the buckle and is moderately tight, then, with both hands, bracing it so that room remains for one finger to be passed between it and the horse. The same must be done in the case of the outer girth.

In a modified degree the side-saddle is displaced by the common mode of girthing. The surcingle should lie neatly over the girths, and have an equal bearing with them. When the "Fitzwilliam girth" is used--and its general use is to be advocated, not only on account of its safety and the firmness of the broad web, but for its freedom from rubbing the skin behind the elbow--the leather surcingle of the saddle will take the place of the usual leather outside strap supplied with this girth.

For inspection the horse should be brought up to the lady, off side on. She should note that the throat-lash falls easily, but not dangling, on the commencement of the curve of the cheek-bone, and that it is not buckled tight round the throttle, like a hangman's "hempen-tow." The bridoon should hang easily in the mouth, clear of the corners or angles, and not wrinkling them; the curb an inch or so above the tusk, or, in the case of a mare, where that tooth might be supposed to be placed. She will see that the curb-chain is not too tight, that the lip-strap is carried through the small ring on the chain, also that the chain lies smooth and even. In fixing the curb, if the chain be turned to the right, the links will unfold themselves. It is taken for granted that by frequent personal visits to the stable, or by trusty deputy, she is satisfied that the horse's back and withers are not galled or wrung. A groom withholding information on this point should, after one warning, get his cong? That the bits and stirrup be burnished as bright as a Life Guardsman's cuirasse, the saddle and bridle perfectly clean, and the horse thoroughly well groomed, goes without saying. All the appointments being found in a condition fit for Queen's escort duty, we now proceed to put the lady in, not into, her saddle. She should approach the horse from the front, and not from behind.

After a kind word or two and a little "gentling," she, with her whip, hunting crop, or riding cane in her right hand, picks up the bridoon rein with her left, draws it through the right smoothly and evenly, feeling the horse's mouth very lightly, until it reaches the crutch, which she takes hold of. In passing the rein through the hand, care must be taken that it is not allowed to slacken so that touch of the mouth is lost. Attention to this will keep the horse in his position whilst being mounted; for should he move backward or forward or away as the lady is in the act of springing into the saddle, he not only makes the vaulting exceedingly awkward, but dangerous. Many horses sidle away as the lady is balanced on one foot and holding on to the pommel with the right hand, in which case she must at once quit her hold or a fall will follow.

Having adjusted the rein of the bridoon to an equal length, the whip point down with the end of the rein on the off side, she stands looking in the direction the horse is standing--i.e., to her proper front, her right shoulder and arm in contact with the flap of the saddle near side. The mounter advances facing her, and, close to the horse's shoulder, can perform his office in three different ways. Stooping down, he places his right hand, knuckles downwards, on his right knee, and of it the lady makes a sort of mounting block, whence, springing from the left foot, she reaches her saddle. When she springs she has the aid of her grip on the crutch, supplemented by the raising power of her left hand resting on the man's shoulder. Or the groom aids the spring by the uplifting of both the hand and the knee. The third method is, for the mounter--his left arm, as before, touching the horse's shoulder--to stoop down till his left shoulder comes within easy reach of the lady's left hand, which she lays on it. He at the same time advances his left foot till it interposes between her and the horse and makes a cradle of his hands, into which she places her left foot. Her grip is still on the crutch, and she still feels the horse's mouth. One, two, three! she springs like feathered Mercury, and he, straightening himself, accentuates the light bound, and straightway she finds herself in the saddle.

It is dangerous to face the mounter in such a position that the spring is made with the rider's back to her horse's side, for in the event of his starting suddenly or "taking ground to her right," an awkward full-length back-fall may result. The foot must be placed firmly in the mounter's hand; during the lift it must not be advanced, but kept under her, and he must not attempt to raise her till her right foot be clear of the ground. The best plan that can be adopted with a horse in the habit of moving away to one side is to stand him against a low wall or paling, or alongside another horse. A quiet, well-trained horse may stand as firm as one of the British squares at Waterloo, or "the thin red line" at Balaclava, for times without number, but from some unforeseen alarm may suddenly start aside. The spring and lift must go together, or the lady may, like Mahomet's coffin, find herself hanging midway. Practice alone can teach the art of mounting lightly and gracefully, and to an active person there is no difficulty.

There is yet another method of mounting which requires considerably more practice--doing away with the services of a mounter,--and that is for the lady to mount herself. In these days, when so many ladies practise gymnastics and athletic exercises generally, there ought to be no difficulty in acquiring this useful habit. The stirrup is let out till it reaches to about a foot from the ground, the pommel is grasped with the right hand, and with a spring the rider is in her seat. The stirrup is then adjusted to its proper length. Unless the horse be very quiet the groom must stand at his head during this process of mounting.

Mounting from a chair or a pair of steps is certainly not an accomplishment I should recommend ladies to indulge in; still, there are occasions when the friendly aid of a low wall, a stile, the bar of a gate, or even a wheelbarrow, comes handy. In such a predicament, take the bridoon across the palm of the left hand, and drawing the bit rein through on each side of the little or third finger till the horse's mouth be felt, place the right foot in the stirrup, grasp the leaping-head with the left and the upright pommel with the right hand, and spring into the saddle, turning round, left about, in so doing. When in the saddle, disengage the right foot from the stirrup and throw the right leg over the upright head.

When the lady is in the saddle, that is, seated on it, not in riding position but before throwing her right leg over the crutch, the groom, without releasing the hold of her foot altogether, adjusts the folds of the habit, care being taken that there is no crease or fold between the right knee and the saddle. This, in the case of a Zenith, is a matter speedily arranged, and, the adjustment being to her satisfaction, she at once pivots on the centre, and raises her right leg into its place over the crutch. The foot is then placed in the stirrup. When a good seat has been acquired, and the rider does not encumber herself with needless underclothing, this arrangement of habit had best be deferred till the horse is in motion; she can then raise herself in the saddle by straightening the left knee, and, drawing herself forward by grasping the pommel with the right hand, arrange the folds to her entire satisfaction with the left.

Attention must be paid to the length of the stirrup, for on it depends greatly the steadiness of the seat. Many ladies are seen riding with a short stirrup; but this is an error, for it destroys the balance, without which there can be no elegance, invariably causes actual cramp and gives a cramped appearance, forces the rider out of the centre of the saddle, so that the weight on the horse's back is unevenly distributed, and displays too much daylight when rising in the trot. On the other hand, too long a stirrup is equally objectionable, as it causes the body to lean unduly over to the near side in order to retain hold of it, depresses and throws back the left shoulder, and destroys the squareness of position. The length of stirrup should be just sufficient that the rider, by leaning her right hand on the pommel, can, without any strain on the instep, raise herself clear of the saddle; this implies that the knee will be only bent sufficiently to maintain the upward pressure of the knee against the concave leaping-head. The stirrup is intended as a support to the foot, not as an appui to ride from; it is not intended to sustain the full weight of the body, and when so misapplied is certain to establish a sore back. I am strongly of opinion that to be in all respects perfect in the equestrian art, a lady should learn, in the first instance, to ride without a stirrup, so as, under any circumstances that may arise, to be able to do without this appendage. Those who aspire to honours in the hunting-field certainly should accustom themselves to dispense with the stirrup, as by so doing they will acquire a closer and firmer seat; moreover, its absence teaches the beginner, better than any other method, to ride from balance, which is the easiest and best form of equitation for both horse and rider. Many horsewomen are under the impression that it is impossible to rise without the aid of the stirrup, but that such is not the case a course of stirrupless training will soon prove. I do not suggest that riding thus should be made a habit, but only strenuously advocate its practice.

A very general fault, and an extremely ugly one among lady riders, is the habit of sticking out the right foot in front of the saddle. It is not only unsightly, but loosens the hold, for if the toe be stuck out under the habit like a flying jib-boom, the leg becomes the bowsprit, and it is impossible for a straightened leg to grip the crutch. Bend the knee well, keep the toe slightly down, and this ugly habit is beyond the pale of possibility. This ungraceful posture may be caused by the pommels being placed so near together that there is not sufficient room for the leg to lie and bend easily, but this excuse will not hold good in the case of the straight-seat-safety-side-saddle, for it has only one pommel or crutch and one leaping-head.

Having got the lady into her saddle, we next attempt so to instruct her that it may be remarked--

"The rider sat erect and fair."--SCOTT.

THE SEAT.

Hitherto, during the process of mounting and settling herself comfortably, the reins have been in the rider's right hand. Now that women can sit square and look straight out and over their horses' ears, much more latitude is permitted in the hold of the reins. It is no longer essential to hold them only in the left hand, for as often as not--always in hunting or at a hand-gallop--both hands are on the bridle. But, as a rule, the left should be the bridle hand, for if the reins be held in the right, and the horse, as horses often will, gets his head down or bores, the right shoulder is drawn forward, and the left knee, as a matter of course, being drawn back from under, loses its upward pressure against the leaping-head, and the safety of the seat is jeopardized. Were the rein to give way the rider would probably fall backwards off the horse over his off-quarter. On the other hand, when the reins are all gathered into the left hand, the harder the horse may take the bit in his teeth, and the lower he may carry his head, the firmer must be the grip of the crutch and the greater the pressure against the leaping-head.

As the reins must not be gathered up all in a bunch, I give the following directions for placing them in the hand. If riding with a snaffle, as always should be the case with beginners, the reins ought to be separated, passing into the hands between the third and fourth fingers, and out over the fore or index-finger, where they are held by the thumb. In the case of bit and bridoon (the bridoon rein has generally a buckle where it joins, whereas that of the bit is stitched), take up the bridoon rein across the inside of the hand, and draw the bit rein through the hand on each side of the little or third finger until the mouth of the horse be gently felt; turn the remainder of the rein along the inside of the hand, and let it fall over the forefinger on to the off-side; place the bridoon rein upon those of the bit, and close the thumb upon them all.

A second plan equally good is, when the horse is to be ridden mainly on the bridoon: the bridoon rein is taken up by the right hand and drawn flatly through on each side of the second finger of the bridle-hand, till the horse's mouth can be felt, when it is turned over the first joint of the forefinger on to the off-side. The bit rein is next taken up and drawn through on each side of the little finger of the bridle-hand, till there is an equal, or nearly equal, length and feeling with the bridoon, and then laid smoothly over the bridoon rein, with the thumb firmly placed as a stopper upon both, to keep them from slipping. A slight pressure of the little finger will bring the bit into play.

Thirdly, when the control is to be entirely from the bit or curb; the bit rein is taken up by the stitching by the right hand within the bridoon rein, and drawn through on each side of the little finger of the left or bridle-hand, until there is a light and even feel on the horse's mouth; it is then turned over the first joint of the forefinger on the off-side. The bridoon rein is next taken up by the buckle, under the left hand, and laid smoothly over the left bit rein, leaving it sufficiently loose to hang over each side of the horse's neck. The thumb is then placed firmly on both reins, as above.

These different manipulations of the reins may be conveniently practised at home with reins attached to an elastic band, the spring of the band answering to the "feel" on the horse's mouth. But, in addition to these various systems of taking up the reins, much has to be learnt in the direction of separating, shortening, shifting, and so forth. With novices the reins constantly and imperceptibly slip, in which case, the ends of the reins hanging over the forefinger of the bridle-hand are taken altogether into the right, the right hand feels the horse's head, while the loosened fingers of the bridle-hand are run up or down the reins, as required, till they are again adjusted to the proper length, when the fingers once more close on them.

In shifting reins to the right hand, to relieve cramp of the fingers, and so forth, the right hand must always pass over the left, and in replacing them the left hand must be placed over the right. In order to shorten any one rein, the right hand is used to pull on that part which hangs beyond the thumb and forefinger. When a horse refuses obedience to the bridle-hand, it must be reinforced by the right. The three first fingers of the right are placed over the bridoon rein, so that the rein passes between the little and third fingers, the end is then turned over the forefinger and, as usual, the thumb is placed upon it. Expertness in these "permutations and combinations" is only to be arrived at by constant practice. They must be performed without stopping the horse, altering his pace, or even glancing at the hands.

The reins must not be held too loose, but tight enough to keep touch of the horse's mouth; and, on the other hand, there must be no attempt to hold on by the bridle, or what is termed to "ride in the horse's mouth." A short rein is objectionable; there must be no "extension motions," no reaching out for a short hold. The proper position for the bridle-hand is immediately opposite the centre of the waist, and about three or four inches from it, that is, on a level with the elbow, and about three or four inches away from the body. The elbow must neither be squeezed or trussed too tightly to the side, nor thrust out too far, but carried easily, inclining a little from the body. According to strict canons, the thumb should be uppermost, and the lower part of the hand nearer the waist than the upper, the wrist a little rounded, and the little finger in a line with the elbow. A wholesome laxity in conforming to these hard-and-fast rules will be found to add to the grace of the rider. Chaque pays chaque guise, and no two horses are alike in the carriage of the head, the sensitiveness of the mouth, and in action. Like ourselves, they all have their own peculiarities.

THE WALK.

The rider is now seated on what--in the case of a beginner--should be an absolutely quiet, good-tempered, and perfectly trained horse. Before schooling her as to seat, we will ask her to move forward at the walk. At first it is better to have the horse led by a leading rein till the d閣utante is accustomed to the motion and acquires some stock of confidence. She must banish from her mind all thoughts of tumbling off. We do not instruct after this fashion:--Lady (after having taken several lessons at two guineas a dozen) loq.: "Well, Mr. Pummell, have I made any good progress?" "Well, I can't say, ma'am," replies the instructor, "as 'ow you rides werry well as yet, but you falls off, ma'am, a deal more gracefuller as wot you did at first." We do not say that falls must not be expected, but in mere hack and park riding they certainly ought to be few and far between. At a steady and even fast walk the merest tyro cannot, unless bent on experiencing the sensation of a tumble, possibly come to the ground. Doubtless the motion is passing strange at first, and the beginner may be tempted to clutch nervously at the pommel of her saddle, a very bad and unsightly habit, and one that, if not checked from the very first, grows apace and remains.

It is during the walk that the seat is formed, and the rider makes herself practically acquainted with the rules laid down on the handling of the reins. A press of the left leg, a light touch of the whip on the off-side, and a "klk" will promptly put the horse in motion. He may toss his head, and for a pace or two become somewhat unsteady; this is not vice but mere freshness, and he will almost immediately settle down into a quick, sprightly step, measuring each pace exactly, and marking regular cadence, the knee moderately bent, the leg, in the case of what Paddy terms "a flippant shtepper," being sharply caught up, appearing suspended in the air for a second, and the foot brought smartly and firmly, without jar, to the ground. This is the perfection of a walking pace. By degrees any nervousness wears off, the rigid trussed appearance gives place to one of pliancy and comparative security, the body loses its constrained stiffness, and begins to conform to and sway with the movements of the horse. The rider, sitting perfectly straight and erect, approaches the correct position, and lays the foundation of that ease and bearing which are absolutely indispensable.

After a lesson or two, if not of the too-timid order, the lady will find herself sitting just so far forward in the saddle as is consistent with perfect ease and comfort, and with the full power to grasp the upright crutch firmly with her right knee; she will be aware of the friendly grip of the leaping-head over her left leg; the weight of her body will fall exactly on the centre of the saddle; her head, though erect, will be perfectly free from constraint, the shoulders well squared, and the hollow of the back gracefully bent in, as in waltzing. This graceful pose of the figure may be readily acquired, throughout the preliminary lessons, and indeed on all occasions when under tuition, by passing the right arm behind the waist, back of the hand to the body, and riding with it in that position. Another good plan, which can only be practised in the riding-school or in some out-of-the-way quiet corner, and then only on a very steady horse, is for the beginner, without relaxing her grip on the crutch and the pressure on the leaping-head, as she sits, to lean or recline back so that her two shoulder-blades touch the hip-bones of the horse, recovering herself and regaining her upright position without the aid of the reins. The oftener this gymnastic exercise is performed the better.

At intervals during the lessons she should also, having dropped her bridle, assiduously practise the extension motions performed by recruits in our military-riding schools. [See Appendix.] The excellent effects of this physical training will soon be appreciated. But, irrespective of the accuracy of seat, suppleness and strength of limb, confidence and readiness these athletic exercises beget, they may, when least expected, save the rider's life. Some of those for whose instruction I have the honour to write, may find themselves placed in a critical situation, when the ability to lie back or "duck" may save them from a fractured skull.

Inclining the body forward is, from the notion that it tends towards security, a fault very general with timid riders. Nothing, however, in the direction of safety, is further from the fact. Should the horse, after a visit to the farrier and the usual senseless free use of the smith's drawing and paring-knife, tread upon a rolling stone and "peck," the lady, leaning forward, is suddenly thrown still further forward, her whole weight is cast upon his shoulders, so he "of the tender foot" comes down and sends his rider flying over his head. A stoop in the figure is wanting in smartness, and is unattractive.

It is no uncommon thing to see ladies sitting on their horses in the form of the letter S, and the effect can hardly be described as charming. This inelegant position, assumed by the lady in the distance, is caused by being placed too much over to the right in the saddle, owing to a too short stirrup. In attempting to preserve the balance, the body from the waist upwards has a strong twisted lean-over to the left, the neck, to counteract this lateral contortion of the spine, being bent over to the right, the whole pose conveying the impression that the rider must be a cripple braced up in surgeon's irons and other appliances. Not less hideous, and equally prevalent, is the habit of sitting too much to the left, and leaning over in that direction several degrees out of the perpendicular. A novice is apt to contract this leaning-seat from the apprehension, existing in the mind of timid riders, that they must fall off from the off rather than from the near side, so they incline away from the supposed danger. Too long a stirrup is sometimes answerable for this crab-like posture. In both of these awkward postures, the seat becomes insecure, and the due exercise of the "aids" impossible. What is understood by "aids" in the language of the schools are the motions and proper application of the bridle-hand, leg, and heel to control and direct the turnings and paces of the horse.

The expression "riding by balance" has been frequently used, and as it is the essence of good horsemanship, I describe it in the words of an expert as consisting in "a foreknowledge of what direction any given motion of the horse would throw the body, and a ready adaptation of the whole frame to the proper position, before the horse has completed his change of attitude or action; it is that disposition of the person, in accordance with the movements of the horse, which preserves it from an improper inclination to one side or the other, which even the ordinary paces of the horse in the trot or gallop will occasion." In brief, it is the automatic inclination of the person of the rider to the body of the horse by which the equilibrium is maintained.

The rider having to some extent perfected herself in walking straight forward, inclining and turning to the right and to the right about, and in executing the same movements to the left, on all of which I shall have a few words to say later, and when she can halt, rein back, and is generally handy with her horse at the walk, she may attempt a slow TROT, and here her sorrows may be said to begin.

THE TROT.

In this useful but trying pace the lady must sit well down on her saddle, rising and falling in unison with the action of the horse, springing lightly but not too highly by the action of the horse coupled with the flexibility of the instep and the knee. As the horse breaks from the walk into the faster pace, it is best not to attempt to rise from the saddle till he has fairly settled down to his trot--better for a few paces to sit back, somewhat loosely, and bump the saddle. The rise from the saddle is to be made as perpendicularly as possible, though a slight forward inclination of the body from the loins, but not with roached-back, may be permitted, and only just so high as to prevent the jar that ensues from the movements of the rider with the horse not being in unison. The return of the body to the saddle must be quiet, light, and unlaboured. Here it is that the practice without a stirrup will stand the novice in good stead.

This pace is the most difficult of all to ladies, and few there be that attain the art of sitting square and gracefully at this gait, and who rise and fall in the saddle seemingly without an effort and without riding too much in the horse's mouth. Most women raise themselves by holding on to the bridle. Instead of rising to the right, so that they can glance down the horse's shoulder, and descending to left, and thus regain the centre of the saddle, they persist in rising over the horse's left shoulder, and come back on to the saddle in the direction of his off-quarter. This twist of the body to the left destroys the purchase of the foot and knee, and unsteadies the position and hands. Though I have sanctioned a slight leaning forward as the horse breaks into his trot, it must not be overdone, for should he suddenly throw up his head his poll may come in violent contact with the rider's face and forehead, causing a blow that may spoil her beauty, if not knock her senseless.

Till the rider can hit off the secret of rising, she will be severely shaken up-- "churned" as a well-known horsewoman describes the jiggiddy-joggoddy motion,--the teeth feel as if they would be shaken out of their sockets, and stitch-in-the-side puts in its unwelcome appearance. Certes, the preliminary lessons are very trying ones, the disarrangement of "the get-up" too awful, the fatigue dreadful, the alarm no trifle. Nothing seems easier, and yet nothing in the art equestrian is so difficult--not to men with their two stirrups, but to women with one only available. What is more grotesque, ridiculous, and disagreeable than a rider rising and falling in the saddle at a greater and lesser speed than that of her horse? And yet, fair reader, if you will have a little patience, a good deal of perseverance, some determination, and will attend to the hints I give, you shall, in due course, be mistress over the difficulty, and rise and fall with perfect ease and exquisite grace, free from all embarras or undue fatigue.

First of all, we must put you on a very smooth, easy, and sedate trotter; by-and-by we may transfer your saddle to something more sharp and lively, perhaps even indulge you with a mount on a regular "bone-setter." To commence with, the lessons, or rather trotting bouts, shall be short, there shall be frequent halts, and during these halts I shall make you drop your reins and put you through extension and balance motions, endeavour to correct your position on the saddle, catechize you closely on the "aids," and introduce as much variety as possible.

Before urging your steed into his wild six or seven-mile-an-hour career, please bear in mind that you must not rise suddenly, or with a jerk, but quietly and smoothly, letting the impetus come from the motion of the horse. The rise from the saddle must not be initiated by a long pull and strong pull at his mouth, a spasmodic grip of your right leg on the crutch, or a violent attempt to raise yourself in the air from your stirrup. The horse will not accommodate his action to yours, you must "take him on the hop," as the saying is. If horse and rider go disjointly, or you do not harmonize your movements with his, then it is something as unpleasant as dancing a waltz with a partner who won't keep time, or rowing "spoonful about."

Falling in with the trot of a horse is at first very difficult. In order to facilitate matters as much as possible, you shall, for a few days, substitute the old-fashioned slipper for the stirrup, as then the spring will come from the toes and not from the hollow of the foot; this will lessen the exertion and be easier. If nature has happened to fashion you somewhat short from the hip to the knee, and you will attend to instruction and practice frequently, the chances are strong in your favour of conquering the irksome "cross-jolt." Separate your reins, taking one in each hand, feeling the mouth equally with both reins, sit well down on your saddle, keep your left foot pointed straight to the front, don't attempt to move till the horse has steadied into his trot, which, in case of a well trained animal, will be in a stride or two, then endeavour, obeying the impulse of his movement, to time the rise.

A really perfectly broken horse, "supplied on both hands," as it is termed, leads, in the trot as in the canter, equally well with either leg, but, in both paces, a very large majority have a favourite leading leg. By glancing over the right shoulder the time for the rise may be taken. Do not be disheartened by repeated failures to "catch on;" persevere, and suddenly you will hit it off. When the least fatigued, pull up into a walk, and when rested have another try. At the risk of repetition, I again impress on you the necessity of keeping the toe of the left foot pointed to the front, the foot itself back, and with the heel depressed. Your descent into the saddle should be such that any one you may be riding straight at, shall see a part of your right shoulder and hip as they rise and fall, his line of vision being directed along the off-side of the horse's neck. When these two portions of your body are so visible then the weight is in its proper place, and there is no fear of the saddle being dragged over the horse's near shoulder. For a few strides there is no objection to your taking a light hold of the pommel with the right hand, in order to time the rise, but the moment the "cross-jolt" ceases, and you find yourself moving in unison with the horse, the hold must be relaxed. Some difficulty will be found in remaining long enough out of the saddle at each rise to avoid descending too soon, and thus receive a double cross-jolt; but this will be overcome after a few attempts. Keep the hands well down and the elbows in.

Varying the speed in the trot will be found excellent practice for the hands; the faster a horse goes, generally speaking, the easier he goes. He must be kept going "well within himself," that is he must not be urged to trot at a greater speed than he can compass with true and equal action. Some very fast trotters, "daisy cutters," go with so little upward jerk that it is almost impossible to rise on them at all. Any attempt at half-cantering with his hind legs must be at once checked by pulling him together, and, by slowing him down, getting him back into collected form. Should he "break" badly, from being over-paced, into a canter or hard-gallop, then rein him in, pulling up, if need be, into a walk, chiding him at the same time. When he again brings his head in and begins to step clean, light, and evenly, then let him resume his trot. If not going up to his bit and hanging heavy on the hand, move the bit in his mouth, let him feel the leg, and talk to him. Like ourselves, horses are not up to the mark every day, and though they do not go to heated theatres and crowded ball-rooms, or indulge as some of their masters and mistresses are said to do, they too often spend twenty hours or more out of the twenty-four in the vitiated atmosphere of a hot, badly ventilated stable, and their insides are converted into apothecaries' shops by ignorant doctoring grooms. When a free horse does not face his bit, he is either fatigued or something is amiss.

THE CANTER.

Properly speaking, this being, par excellence, the lady's pace, the instruction should precede that of the trot. The comparative ease of the canter, and the readiness with which the average pupil takes to it, induces the beginner to at once indulge in it. It is, on a thoroughly trained horse, so agreeable that the uninitiated at once acquire confidence on horseback. Moreover, it is the pace at which a fine figure and elegant lady-like bearing is most conspicuously displayed, and for this, if for no other reason, the pupil applies herself earnestly--shall I say lovingly?--to perfect herself in this delightful feature of the art. On a light-actioned horse, one moving as it were on springs, going well on his haunches, and well up to this bit, the motion is as easy as that of a rocking-chair. All the rider has to do is to sit back, keep the body quite flexible and in the centre of the saddle, preserve the balance, and, with pressure from the left leg and heel, and a touch of the whip, keep him up to his bit. She will imperceptibly leave the saddle at every stride, which, in a slow measured canter, will be reduced to a sort of rubbing motion, just sufficient to ease the slight jolt caused by the action of the haunches and hind legs.

Many park-horses and ladies' hacks are trained to spring at once, without breaking into a run or trot, into the canter. All the rider has to do is to raise the hand ever so little, press him with the leg, touch him with the whip, and give him the unspellable signal "klk." The movement or sway of the body should follow that of the horse. As soon as he is in his stride, the rider throws back her body a little, and places her hand in a suitable position. If the horse carries his head well, the hand ought to be about three inches from the pommel, and at an equal distance from the body. For "star-gazers" it should be lower; and for borers it should be raised higher. Once properly under way the lady will study that almost imperceptible willow-like bend of the back, her shoulders will be thrown back gracefully, the mere suspicion of a swing accommodating itself to the motion of the horse will come from the pliant waist, and she will yield herself just a little to the opposite side from that the horse's leading leg is on. If he leads with the off-foot, he inclines a trifle to the left, and the rider's body and hands must turn but a little to the left also, and vice versâ?

It is the rider's province to direct which foot the horse shall lead with. To canter with the left fore leg leading, the extra bearing will be upon the left rein, the little finger turned up towards the right shoulder, the hint from the whip--a mere touch should suffice--being on the right shoulder or flank. It is essential that the bearing upon the mouth, a light playing touch, should be preserved throughout the whole pace. If the horse should, within a short distance--say a mile or so,--flag, then he must be reminded by gentle application of the whip. He cannot canter truly and bear himself handsomely unless going up to his bit. The rider must feel the cadence of every pace, and be able to extend or shorten the stride at will. It is an excellent plan to change the leading leg frequently, so that upon any disturbance of pace, going "false," or change of direction, the rider may be equal to the occasion. The lady must be careful that the bridle-arm does not acquire the ugly habit of leaving the body and the elbow of being stuck out of it akimbo. All the movements of the hand should proceed from the wrist, the bearings and play on the horse's mouth being kept up by the little finger.

Ladies will find that most horses are trained to lead entirely with the off leg, and that when, from any disturbance of pace, they are forced to "change step" and lead with the near leg, their action becomes very awkward and uneven. Hence they are prone to regard cantering with the near leg as disagreeable. But when they come to use their own horses, they will find it good economy to teach them to change the leading leg constantly, both during the canter and at the commencement of the pace. To make a horse change foot in his canter, if he cannot be got readily to do so by hand, leg, and heel, turn him to the right, as if to circle, and he will lead with the off foreleg, and by repeating the same make-believe manoeuvre to the left, the near fore will be in front. The beginner, however, had better pull up into the walk before attempting this change. When pulling up from the canter, it is best and safest to let the horse drop into a trot for a few paces and so resume the walk.

There is no better course of tuition by which to acquire balance than the various inclinations to the right and left, the turns to the right and left and to the right and left-about at the canter, all of which, with the exception of the full turns, should be performed on the move without halting. In the turn-about, it is necessary to bring the horse to a momentary halt before the turn be commenced, and so soon as he has gone about and the turn is fully completed, a lift of the hand and a touch of the leg and heel should instanter compel him to move forward at the canter in the opposite direction; he must no sooner be round than off. When no Riding-school is available, one constructed of hurdles closely laced with gorse, on the sheep-lambing principle, will answer all purposes. Should the horse be at all awkward or unsteady, the hurdles, placed one on the top of the other and tied to uprights driven into the ground, closely interlaced with the gorse so that he cannot see through or over the barrier, will form a perfect, retired exercise ground. A plentiful surface dressing of golden-peat-moss-litter will save his legs and feet. In a quiet open impromptu school of this description, away from "the madding crowd," I have schooled young horses so that they would canter almost on their own ground, circling round a bamboo lance shaft, the point in the ground and the butt in my right hand, without changing legs or altering pace, and they would describe the figure eight with almost mathematical precision, changing leg at every turn without any "aid" from me, a mere inclination of the body bringing them round the curves. A horse very handy with his legs can readily change them at the corners when making the full right-angle turn, but there is always at first the danger of one not so clever attempting to execute the turn by crossing the leading leg over the supporting one, when the rider will be lucky to get off with an awkward stumble--a "cropper" will most likely follow. When at this private practice, "make much of your horse"--that is, caress and speak kindly to him, when he does well; in fact, the more he is spoken to throughout the lesson, the better for both parties. So good and discriminating is a horse's ear that he soon learns to appreciate the difference between kindly approval and stern censure. A sympathy between horse and rider is soon established, and such freemasonry is delightful.

Never canter on the high road, and see that your groom does not indulge himself by so doing. On elastic springy turf the pace, which in reality is a series of short bounds, if not continued too long at a time, does no great harm, but one mile on a hard, unyielding surface causes more wear-and-tear of joints, shoulders, and frame generally, than a long day's work of alternating walk and trot which, on the Queen's highway, are the proper paces. There is no objection to a canter when a bit of turf is found on the road-side; and the little drains cut to lead the water off the turnpike into the ditch serve to make young horses handy with their legs.

THE HAND-GALLOP AND GALLOP.

The rider should not attempt either of these accelerated paces till quite confident that she has the horse under complete control. As the hand-gallop is only another and quickened form of the canter, in which the stride is both lengthened and hastened, or, more correctly speaking, in which the bounds are longer and faster, the same rules are applicable to both. Many horses, especially those through whose veins strong hot blood is pulsing, fairly revel in the gallop, and if allowed to gain upon the hand, will soon extend the hand-gallop to full-gallop, and that rapid pace into a runaway. The rider must, therefore, always keep her horse well in hand, so as to be able to slacken speed should he get up too much steam. Some, impatient of restraint, will shake their heads, snatch at their bits, and yaw about, "fighting for their heads," as it is termed, and will endeavour to bore and get their heads down.

A well-trained horse, one such as a beginner should ride, will not play these pranks and will not take a dead pull at the rider's hands; on the contrary, he will stride along quite collectedly, keeping his head in its proper place, and taking just sufficient hold to make things pleasant. But horses with perfect mouths and manners are, like angels' visits, few and far between, and are eagerly sought after by those fortunate beings to whom money is no object. To be on the safe side, the rider should always be on the alert and prepared to at once apply the brake. When fairly in his stride and going comfortably, the rider, leaning slightly forward, should, with both hands on the bridle, give and take with each stroke, playing the while with the curb; she should talk cheerily to him, but the least effort on his part to gain upon the hand must be at once checked. The play of the little fingers on the curb keeps his mouth alive, prevents his hanging or boring, and makes it sensible to the rider's hand.

"Keeping a horse in hand" means that there is such a system of communication established between the rider and the quadruped that the former is mistress of the situation, and knows, almost before the horse has made up his mind what to do, what is coming. This keeping in hand is one of the secrets of fine horsemanship, and it especially suits the light-hearted mercurial sort of goer, one that is always more or less off the ground or in the air, one of those that "treads so light he scarcely prints the plain."

My impression is, despite the numerous bits devised and advertised to stop runaways, that nothing short of a long and steep hill, a steam-cultivated, stiff clay fallow, or the Bog of Allen, will stop the determined bolt of a self-willed, callous-mouthed horse. There is no use pulling at him, for the more you pull the harder he hardens his heart and his mouth. The only plan, if there be plenty of elbow room, is to let him have his wicked way a bit, then, with one mighty concentrated effort to give a sudden snatch at the bit, followed by instantly and rapidly drawing, "sawing," of the bridoon through his mouth. Above all, keep your presence of mind, and if by any good luck you can so pilot the brute as to make him face an ascent, drive him up it--if it be as steep as the roof of a house, so much the better,--plying whip and spur, till he be completely "pumped out" and dead beat. Failing a steep hill, perhaps a ploughed field may present itself, through and round which he should be ridden, in the very fullest sense of the word, till he stands still. Such a horse is utterly unfit to carry a lady, and, should she come safe and sound out of the uncomfortable ride, he had better be consigned to Tattersall's or "The Lane," to be sold "absolutely without reserve."

Worse still than the runaway professional bolter is the panic-stricken flight of a suddenly scared horse, in which abject terror reigns supreme, launching him at the top of his speed in full flight from some imaginary foe. Nature has taught him to seek safety in flight, and the frightened animal, with desperate and exhausting energy, will gallop till he drops. Professor Galvayne's system claims to be effective with runaway and nervous bolters. At Ayr that distinguished horse-tamer cured, in the space of one hour, an inveterate performer in that objectionable line, and a pair he now drives were, at one time, given to like malpractices.

Do not urge your horse suddenly from a canter into a full gallop; let him settle down to his pace gradually--steady him. Being jumped off, like a racehorse with a flying start at the fall of the flag, is very apt to make a hot, high-couraged horse run away or attempt to do so. Some horses, however, allow great liberties to be taken with them, and others none. All depends on temperament, and whether the nervous, fibrous, sanguine, or lymphatic element preponderates. And here let me remark that the fibrous temperament is the one to struggle and endure, to last the longest, and to give the maximum of ease, comfort, and satisfaction to owner and rider.

LEAPING.

"Throw the broad ditch behind you; o'er the hedge High bound, resistless; nor the deep morass refuse."

THOMPSON.

Though the "pleasures of the chase" are purposely excluded from this volume, the horsewoman's preliminary course of instruction would hardly be complete without a few remarks on jumping. In clearing an obstacle, a horse must to all intents and purposes go through all the motions inherent to the vices of rearing, plunging, and kicking, yet the three, when in rapid combination, are by no means difficult to accommodate one's self to. It is best to commence on a clever, steady horse--"a safe conveyance" that will go quietly at his fences, jump them without an effort, landing light as a cork, and one that will never dream of refusing. As beginners, no matter what instructors may say and protest, will invariably, for the first few leaps, till they acquire confidence, grip, and balance, ride to some extent "in the horse's mouth," they should be placed on an animal with not too sensitive a mouth, one that can go pleasantly in a plain snaffle.

Begin with something low, simple, and easy--say a three feet high gorsed hurdle, so thickly laced with the whin that daylight cannot be seen through, with a low white-painted rail some little distance from it on the take-off side. If there be a ditch between the rail and the fence, so much the better, for the more the horse spreads himself the easier it will be to the rider, the jerk or prop on landing the less severe. Some horses sail over the largest obstacle, land, and are away again without their appearing to call upon themselves for any extra exertion; they clear it in their stride. Hunters that know their business can be trotted up to five-barred gates and stiff timber, which they will clear with consummate ease; but height and width require distinct efforts, and the rear and kick in this mode of negotiating a fence are so pronounced and so sudden that they would be certain to unseat the novice.

It is easiest to sit a leap if the horse is ridden at it in a canter or, at most, in a well-collected, slow hand-gallop. The reins being held in both hands with a firm, steady hold, the horse should be ridden straight at the spot you have selected to jump. Sit straight, or, if anything out of the perpendicular, lean a little back. The run at the fence need only be a few yards. As he nears it, the forward prick of his alert ears and a certain measuring of his distance will indicate that he means "to have it," and is gathering himself for the effort. The rider should then, if she can persuade herself so to do, give him full liberty of head. Certain instructors, and horsemen in general, will prate glibly of "lifting" a horse over his fence. I have read of steeplechase riders "throwing" their horses over almost unnegotiable obstacles, but it is about as easy to upend an elephant by the tail and throw him over the garden wall as it is for any rider to "lift" his horse. Although the horse must be made to feel, as he approaches the fence, that it is utterly impossible for him to swerve from it, yet the instant he is about to rise the reins should be slacked off, to be almost immediately brought to bear again as he descends.

Irish horses are the best jumpers we have, and their excellence may justly be ascribed to the fact that, for the most part, they are ridden in the snaffle bridle. If the horse be held too light by the head he will "buck over" the obstacle, a form of jumping well calculated to jerk the beginner out of her saddle. After topping the hurdle, the horse's forehand, in his descent, will be lower than his hind quarters. Had the rider leant forward as he rose on his hind legs, the violent effort or kick of his haunches would have thrown her still further over his neck, whereas, having left the ground with a slight inclination towards the croup, the forward spring of the horse will add to that backward tendency and place her in the best possible position in which to counteract the shock received upon his forefeet reaching the ground. If the rider does not slacken the reins as the horse makes his spring, they must either be drawn through her hands or she will land right out on his neck.

I have referred to the "buck-over" system of jumping, which is very common with Irish horses. A mare of mine, well-known in days of yore at Fermoy as "Up-she-rises," would have puzzled even Mrs. Power O'Donoghue. She would come full gallop, when hounds were running, at a stone wall, pull up and crouch close under it, then, with one mighty effort, throw herself over, her hind legs landing on the other side little more than the thickness of the wall from where her forefeet had taken off. It was not a "buck," but a straight up-on-end rear, followed by a frantic kick that threatened to hurl saddle and rider half across the field. "Scrutator," in "Horses and Hounds," makes mention of an Irish horse, which would take most extraordinary leaps over gates and walls, and if going ever so fast would always check himself and take his leaps after his own fashion. "Not thinking him," writes this fine sportsman, "up to my weight, he was handed over to the second whipper-in, and treated

Jack at first acquaintance to a rattling fall or two. He rode him, as he had done his other horses, pretty fast at a stiff gate, which came in his way the first day. Some of the field, not fancying it, persuaded Jack to try first, calculating upon his knocking it open, or breaking the top bar. The horse, before taking off, stopped quite short, and jerked him out of the saddle over to the other side; then raising himself on his hind legs, vaulted over upon Jack, who was lying on his back. Not being damaged, Jack picked himself up, and grinning at his friends, who were on the wrong side laughing at his fall, said, 'Never mind, gentlemen, 'tis a rum way of doing things that horse has; but no matter, we are both on the right side, and that's where you won't be just yet.'"

The standing jump is much more difficult, till the necessary balance be acquired, than the flying leap. The lower and longer the curve described, the easier to sit; but in this description of leaping, the horse, though he clears height, cannot cover much ground. His motion is like that of the Whip's horse described above, and the rider will find the effort, as he springs from his haunches, much more accentuated than in the case of the flying leap, and therefore the more difficult to sit. As, however, leaping, properly speaking, belongs to the hunting-field, I propose to deal more fully with the subject in another volume.

DISMOUNTING.

When the novice dismounts there should, at first, be two persons to aid-- one to hold the horse's head, the other to lift her from the saddle. After a very few lessons, if the lady be active and her hack a steady one, the services of the former may be dispensed with. Of course the horse is brought to full stop. Transfer the whip to the left hand, throw the right leg over to the near side of the crutch and disengage the foot from the stirrup. Let the reins fall on the neck, see that the habit skirt is quite clear of the leaping-head, turn in the saddle, place the left hand upon the right arm of the cavalier or squire, the right on the leaping-head, and half spring half glide to the ground, lighting on the balls of the feet, dropping a slight curtsey to break the jar on the frame.

Retain hold of the leaping-head till safely landed.

Very few men understand the proper manner in which to exercise the duties of the cavalier servant in mounting and dismounting ladies. Many ladies not unreasonably object to be lifted off their horses almost into grooms' arms. A correspondent of the Sporting and Dramatic News mentions a contretemps to a somewhat portly lady in the Crimea, whose husband, in hoisting her up on to her saddle with more vigour than skill, sent his better half right over the horse's back sprawling on the ground. It is by no means an uncommon thing to see ladies, owing to want of lift on the part of the lifter and general clumsiness, failing to reach the saddle and slipping down again.

Having dismounted, "make much" of your horse, and give him a bit of carrot, sugar, apple, or some tid-bit. Horses are particularly fond of apples.

CHAPTER IV.

THE SIDE SADDLE.

It is of first-class importance that a lady's saddle should be made by a respectable and thoroughly competent saddler. Seeing the number of years a well-built and properly kept side-saddle will last, it is but penny wise to grudge the necessary outlay in the first instance. Those constructed on the cheap machine-made system never give satisfaction to the rider, are constantly in need of repair (grooms, if permitted, are everlastingly in and out of the saddler's shop), and are a prolific cause of sore backs.

With all saddles the chief cause, the source and origin, of evil is badly constructed and badly fitting trees that take an undue bearing on different parts of the back. At a critical moment, when just a little extra exertion would perhaps keep the horse on his legs, a somewhat tender muscle or portion of "scalded" skin comes in painful contact with some part of an ill-fitting saddle, the agony causing him to wince, checks the impulse to extend the "spare leg," and he comes down. It does not matter how hard or heavy the rider may be, how tender the skin, a sore back can be prevented by a proper system of measurement and a good pannel. Mrs. Power O'Donoghue, in her very interesting letters upon "Ladies on Horseback," unsparingly condemns the elaborate embroidery which adorned (?) the near flap of every old-fashioned saddle, pointing out that as it is always concealed by the rider's right leg, the work is a needless expense. "There might be some sense," that brilliant and bold horsewoman says, "although very little, in decorating the off-side and imparting to it somewhat of an ornamental appearance; but in my opinion there cannot be too much simplicity about anything connected with riding appointments. Let your saddle, like your personal attire, be remarkable only for perfect freedom from ornament or display. Have it made to suit yourself-- neither too weighty nor yet too small,--and if you want to ride with grace and comfort, desire that it be constructed without one particle of the objectionable dip."

The foregoing two sketches, "The Old Style" and "The Straight-Seated Safety," contrast the wide difference between the old and fast disappearing form of side-saddle and that designed and manufactured by Messrs. Champion and Wilton. The disadvantages of the old style are so painfully obvious that it is marvellous they should not have been remedied years ago. On, or rather in, one of these, the lady sat in a dip or kind of basin, and unless her limbs were of unusual length--thereby pushing her right knee towards the off-side--she necessarily faced half-left, both, not her horse's ears, but his near shoulder; or, in order to attain any squareness of front, she was called upon to twist her body from the hips, and to maintain a most fatiguing, forced position during her whole ride (even through a long day's hunting), or else sit altogether on the near side of her saddle. This twist was the cause of the pains in the spine so frequently complained of. More than this, the height upon which her pommels were raised caused her to sit, as it were, uphill, or at best (in the attempt on the part of the saddler to rectify this, by stuffing up the seat of her saddle) to find herself perched far above her horse's back. The natural expedient of carrying the upper or middle pommel nearer the centre of the horse's withers, so as to bring the knee about in a line with his mane, was impracticable with the old-style of saddle tree, which gave the pommels a lofty, arched base above the apex of his shoulders. The result was, in all cases, (1) great inconvenience and often curvature of the spine to the rider, (2) constant liability to sore back on the part of the horse, through the cross friction produced by the lady's one-sided position. To meet and entirely remove the difficulty, Messrs. Champion and Wilton pruned away all the forepart of the saddle-tree, and, in place of the raised wood and metal base, upon which the lady's right leg formerly rested, substituted merely a stout leather flap or cushion.

As will be seen from the foregoing illustration, they were by this arrangement able to place the upper pommel in whatever exact position the form of the rider may require, to enable her to sit straight to her proper front, riding the whole upon a level seat, and distributing her weight fairly upon her horse's back. The importance of being in a position to face her work and to hold her horse at his, needs no comment. The small holster attached to the saddle is an exceedingly ingenious air and water-tight detachable receptacle for a reliable watch with a very clearly marked dial. The rider thus always has the time before her eyes, and is saved the great inconvenience--in the hunting-field especially--of unbuttoning the habit to get out a watch. This invention, though not a necessity, is a very handy adjunct.

This superlatively good saddle is fitted with a PATENT SAFETY-STIRRUP BAR, which, while it renders it impossible for the rider to be hung up or dragged when thrown, cannot possibly become detached so long as she remains in the saddle. The action of this perfect safeguard is explained by the accompanying diagrams.

The back of the bar is fixed to the tree in the ordinary way. There are only two moving parts, viz. the hinged hook-piece, marked A, Figs. 1, 2, and 3, upon which the loop of the stirrup-leather is hung, and the locking bar, B, upon which the skirt and the rider's legs rest. It will be noticed that the front of the hook-piece, marked A, Fig. 1, is cut off diagonally front and back, and that there is upon the back-plate a cone, marked C, which projects through the back of the hook-piece. The locking action may be thus described: The skirt, with lever, B, Fig. 2, is lifted, the hook, A, pulled forward, and the loop of the stirrup-leather hooked upon it; it springs back again (spring not shown) and the locking lever, B, falls down over it, as at Fig 3. While in the saddle, one of the rider's legs rests at all times upon the skirt and lever, which therefore cannot rise; but upon the rider being thrown and dragged, the stirrup-leather is tilted diagonally against the cone, C, in passing which the hook is thrust outwards, lifting the locking lever and skirt, as shown, Fig. 2, and thus reaching the releasing point, is free. There is another case more rare, that in which the rider is thrown over the horse's head, and also over a gate or fence when the horse refuses and backs; and here we have just the reverse action to that of the ordinary dragging, but in this case the bar acts equally well. When the rider is thrown and dragged on the off or reverse side, the stirrup-leather lifts the skirt and locking lever, Fig. 2, and there remains nothing to retain the loop to the bar. The above sketch of the side-saddle will aid in making the foregoing clear. Here A is the skirt, and locking lever, B, shown raised, in order to fit the loop of the stirrup-leather to the hook C below the cone D.

A balance strap is usually supplied with a side-saddle, and is a very desirable adjunct. Ds also, to which the cover-coat is attached, should be fitted on.

Quilted or plain doeskin seat and pommels are matters of taste. These extras add to the cost of the saddle. A waterproof or leather cover is an essential. Hogskin caps and straps, to prevent the habit catching on the pommels, should be provided when the new patent safety-bar stirrup is not used.

When practicable a lady should invariably be measured for her saddle. It is almost impossible to find a lady's horse that at some time or another has not suffered from sore back, and it is imperative that the saddle should fit both and that perfectly. We bipeds cannot walk or run in tight ill-fitting boots, neither can a horse act under a badly fitting saddle. I have read somewhere that the Empress of Austria rode in an 8-lb. saddle, a statement I take leave to doubt. Her Imperial Highness is far too fine and experienced a horsewoman to have been seen outside any such toy. In the present day there is a senseless rage for light side-saddles, much to be deprecated, as the lightness is gained at the expense of the tree, and light flimsy leather is used in their manufacture. Possibly when alum comes into general use we may see lighter and even strong trees. A lady weighing 9 stone 7 lbs. requires a saddle about 17 inches long, measured, as in the sketch, from A to B, the seat from C to D, 13-1/4 inches wide, the upright pommel 5-1/2 inches high, and the leaping-head 8 inches long. Such a saddle, brand new, will weigh about 14 lbs., and at the end of a season will pull the scale down at 18 to 20 lbs. A saddle made of the proper weight and strength in the first instance--the extra weight being in the tree, where the strength is required--will be lighter in appearance.

Light saddles always require a lot of extra stuffing, which soon mounts up the weight and detracts from the looks; moreover it is very inconvenient to be constantly sending one's saddle to be restuffed. Most ladies, from lack of proper supervision and want of thought, are neglectful of the make and condition of their saddles, and so some ribald cynic has hazarded the remark that although "a good man is merciful to his beast, a good woman is rarely so." A first class firm keeps an experienced man for the purpose of measuring horses, who is sent out any distance required at a fixed scale of charges. When a lady cannot conveniently attend to be measured, she should endeavour to get the measurements, as indicated in the sketch, from some saddle in which she can ride with comfort.

Though careful fitting and adjustment of the saddle will reduce friction to a minimum, and will, in the majority of cases, do away with its baneful effects, still with some very highly bred horses the skin of the back is so easily irritated, that during a long day's work, in hot climates especially, it becomes chafed, and injury is inflicted either at the withers or underneath the seat. Nothing is more difficult to deal with and heal than a sore back. In a prolonged and arduous campaign, I have seen regiments seriously reduced below their fighting strength by obstinate sore backs. A very great desideratum, in my opinion, is the new "Humanity" sponge-lined numnah, another of Messrs. Champion and Wilton's sensible inventions. This excellent preventative and curative Saddle-cloth keeps the most tender-skinned horse in a position to walk in comfort. It is an adaptation of the finer kind of Turkey sponge, the soft nature of which suggested itself to the inventors as an agent for counteracting saddle friction.

It is made in two varieties: (1) of bridle leather, lined at the withers with this fine, natural sponge, thus interposing a soft pad between the saddle and the withers (a point where the chief strain of a lady's seat is brought to bear during the action of the trot); (2) of a fine white felt, lined at the back as well as at the withers with the same quality of sponge, and intended for such horses as are apt to become troubled under the seat of the saddle as well as at the withers. The sponge has to be damped, preferably in warm water, but pressed or wrung out before using, and the leather part kept soft with vaseline, which is an excellent preservative and softener of leather. Each time after use, the sweat should be thoroughly washed out of the sponge; to ensure best results, attention to scrupulous cleanliness is absolutely essential. The following are representations of this numnah.

With the safety-bar and the Zenith habit it matters not what form of stirrup a lady uses, for these have done away with the necessity for the so-called safety patterns, of which there are several. The slipper has been objected to, as it, from being so comfortable, encourages ladies to lean their whole weight on it and thus throw themselves out of balance; moreover, it is out of fashion. Mrs. Power O'Donoghue advocates the plain iron racing stirrup, with the foot well home, as by its means the rise or purchase is from the instep, as it ought to be, and not from the toes. The Prussian side-pieces at the bottom take sharp pressure off the sides of the foot. The Victoria and French pad inside the stirrup, except when the safety bar and habit are adopted, are fraught with danger; with these precautions they are a great comfort, and guard the instep at the trot when the foot is thrust well home. The size of the stirrup should be proportionate to the foot.

CHAPTER V.

HINTS UPON COSTUME.

"She wore what was then somewhat universal--a coat, vest, and hat resembling those of a man; which fashion has since called a RIDING-HABIT."-- Diana Vernon, SCOTT.

Under no circumstances does a lady, possessed of good figure and carriage, appear to such great advantage, or is she so fascinating, as when with mien and bearing haught and high, with perfect, well-balanced seat, and light hands, faultlessly appointed, firmly, gently, and with seeming carelessness she controls some spirited high-bred horse, some noble steed of stainless purity of breed, whose rounded symmetry of form, characteristic spring of the tail, and pride of port, proclaim his descent from

"The Silver Arab with his purple veins, The true blood royal of his race."

At no time are the beauties of the female form divine displayed with such witching grace, the faultless flowing lines so attractively posed, the tout ensemble so thoroughly patrician. But if there be one blot in the fair picture the whole charm at once vanishes. The incomparable dignity, the well-turned-out steeds--the best that money could buy or critical judgment select--the perfect figure of that superb horsewoman the Empress of Austria, of whom it may justly be said "All the pride of all her race in herself reflected lives," were it possible for Her Imperial Majesty to err in such a matter, would have been of little effect, but for a faultlessly cut and fitting habit.

"Fine feathers make fine birds," and though in riding costume the plumage, save in the hunting-field, must be of sombre tint, it must be unruffled and lie perfectly flat. There are Habit-makers and Habit-makers; a very few as perfect as need be, more mediocre, most arrant bunglers. Of late years legions of so-called ladies'-tailors have sprung into being, not one in a hundred possessing the faintest idea of what is wanted. A Habit-maker is a genius not often met with, and when come across should be made a note of. A perfect fitting habit, though not quite "a joy for ever," is a very useful, long-wearing, and altogether desirable garment. Particular attention must be given to the cutting of the back of the neck to secure plenty of play, and to prevent that disagreeable tightness so often experienced, which completely mars the easy and graceful movement of the head. While giving absolute freedom to the figure, the well shaped body will fit like a glove. A tight habit gives a stiff, inelegant appearance to the whole figure, and produces a feeling of being "cribbed, cabined, and confined," tantamount to semi-suffocation. A too long waist is certain to ride-up and wrinkle. For winter wear there is nothing like the double-breasted body. The choice to select from is a wide one.

To my mind and eye no one understands the whole art of habit-making so well as Mr. W. Shingleton, 60, New Bond Street, London, the inventor of the patent "Zenith" skirt, an ingenious arrangement which should be universally patronized for its absolute safety, if for no less weighty reason. Any lady wearing this clever and smart combination of skirt and trousers, seated on one of Messrs. Champion and Wilton's safety side-saddles, may set her mind completely at rest as to the possibility of being "hung up" on the pommel, or dragged by it or the stirrup. Perfect freedom in the saddle is secured to the rider, that portion of the skirt which in the ordinary habit fits over the pommel, always a source of danger, being entirely dispensed with. The "Zenith" is made in two breadths or portions, instead of three, as heretofore, and on one side this skirt is attached to the trousers at the "side seam" of the right leg, or leg which passes over the pommel. The skirt is then carried across or over both legs of the trousers in front, and, on the other side, is brought round and attached to the "leg seam" of the left leg and to the "seat seam," both the trousers and the skirt being then secured to the waistband. Thus the rider, as stated above, has the pommel leg free to be readily disengaged from the pommel without the skirt catching thereon, the right leg at the back being left uncovered by the skirt. An opening formed on the left side of the skirt allows of the garment being readily put on. The front draping of the skirt remains unaltered from the usual skirt, but when seen from behind it presents the appearance of one leg covered, the other uncovered. When walking, the back of the right trousers leg, which is uncovered, can be draped somewhat by the front of the skirt being lifted and brought round by the right hand. There is nothing whatever in this invention to offend the most sensitive equestrienne, nothing to hurt the proper feelings of the most modest. If preferred, the skirt may be provided on each side with a slit, extending down from the knees, so as to enable the wearer to readily use the skirt when wearing breeches or riding boots. That such an enterprising firm as Messrs. Redfern, of Paris, should have secured the patent rights for France, speaks volumes in favour of Mr. Shingleton's really admirable invention.

Except for summer wear in early morning or in the country, and in the case of young girls, when grey is permissible, the habit should be made of some dark cloth. In the hunting-field, on which subject I am not touching in this volume, some ladies who "go" don pink, those patronising the Duke of Beaufort's wearing the becoming livery of the Badminton Hunt, than which nothing is more becoming. Diagonal ribbed cloths are much in vogue for skirts. Stout figures tone down the appearance of too great solidity and rotundity by wearing an adaptation of the military tunic. The long jacket-body, depicted in Mr. Shingleton's sketch of the "Zenith," is well suited to full figures. Waistcoats are all the rage,--blue bird's-eye, plush-leather with pearl buttons, kersey, corduroy, nankeen, etc., in endless variety, and are very much in evidence, as are shirt fronts, high collars, silk ties with sporting-pin ala cavaliere. Braiding or ornamentation is bad form; no frilling, no streamers are admissible; everything, to be in good taste, ought to be of the very best, without one inch of superfluous material,--severely simple.

In the Park, except for young ladies just entering on their teens, or children, the tall silk hat is de rigueur. The present prevailing "chimney-pot" or "stove-pipe" model, shaped something like the tompion of a gun, is an unbecoming atrocity. Let us hope that fashion will soon revert to the broad curled brim bell-shaped Hardwicke. Nothing is cheap that's bad, and nothing detracts more from the general effect of a "get-up" than a bad hat. So if my lady reader wants to be thoroughly well hatted, let her go to Ye Hatterie, 105, Oxford Street, and be measured for one of Mr. Heath's best. It will last out two or three of other makers, and having done duty one season in Rotten Row, will look well later on in the wear-and-tear of the hunting field, preserving its bright glossy brilliancy, no matter what the weather be. Order a quilted silk lining in preference to a plain leather one, and, when being measured, let the chevelure be compact and suited for riding. A low-crowned hat is the best. For young girls, and out of the season, riding melon-shaped or pot-hats of felt are useful and by no means unbecoming. Mr. Heath makes a speciality of these, and has scores of different, and more or less becoming, styles to select from. Hats made to the shape of the head require no elastics to hold them on, and are not the fruitful source of headache which ready-made misfits invariably are. There is no objection to a grey felt with grey gauze veil in the summer, but black with a black veil is in better taste. Anything in the way of colour, other than grey, or, perhaps brown, is inadmissible. I am not sufficient of a Monsieur Mantalini to advise very minutely on such important points as the ladies' toilette, as to what veils may or may not be worn, but a visit to the Park any morning or forenoon, when London is in Town, will best decide. For dusty roads gauze is essential.

Of all abominations and sources of equestrian discomfort a badly built pair of riding-breeches are the worst. No breeches, pants, or trousers can possibly sit well and give absolute comfort in the saddle without flexible hips and belt-band riding-drawers. The best material, and preferable to all silk, is a blend of silk and cashmere, which wears well, is warm, elastic, of permanent elasticity, can be worn with great comfort by the most sensitive, and is not too expensive. A habit should fit like a glove over the hips, and the flexible-hip make of riding-drawers which I advocate, aids in securing this moulding. The fit of the breeches or pants, especially that of the right leg, at the inside of the knee, should be particularly insisted upon. First-class ladies' tailors generally have a model horse on which their customers can mount when trying on. At Messrs. E. Tautz and Sons' establishment, where the rider can be accoutred to perfection, ladies will find a competent assistant of their own sex,--a trained fitter--who will by careful measurement and subsequent "trying on" secure them against the galling miseries of badly cut and ill-fitting breeches. Materials of every description are available; but if the fair reader will be advised by me, she will select brown undressed deer-skin, which is soft, pliable, and durable. The waistbands and continuations are of strong twilled silk. Leggings are generally and preferably worn with the breeches, and can be had in all shades of cloth to go with the habit.

For the colonies and India a new material, known as Dr. Lahmann's cotton-wool underclothing, cannot be too highly commended. In "the gorgeous East," of which abode of the sun I have had some experience, between March and the latter days of October, the thinnest animal-wool is unbearably warm, and, when prickly-heat is about, absolutely unbearable, the irritation produced by the two being, I should imagine, akin to that endured by the four-footed friend of man when suffering acutely from the mange. Moreover, in the clutches of the Indian dhobie (washerman), woollen materials rapidly shrink by degrees and become beautifully less, when not knocked into holes, and are converted into a species of felt.

This fabric is a new departure in the manufacture of cotton. From first to last it is treated as wool, is spun as wool, and woven as wool, and in my opinion is the best possible material for under wear in the tropics. It is cool, wears well, washes well, is warranted not to shrink, does not irritate the most sensitive skin, and, being woven on circular knitting looms, is peculiarly adapted for close-fitting riding-drawers and under-clothing generally. It has the additional merits of having the appearance and colour of silk--a soft cream colour,--is entirely free from dressing, and is moderate in price. As this fabric (porous, knitted, woven, ribbed, or double-ribbed) is sold by the yard as well as made up into seamless pants, jersies, etc., it is admirably suited to the make of flexible-hip and belt-band drawers referred to above. I feel that in directing attention to this "baumwoll" (tree wool) clothing, I am conferring a benefit on all Europeans whose avocations keep them within the tropics, and on those of them especially who are obliged to take constant and prolonged horse exercise. It is to be obtained at the Lahmann Agency, 15, Fore Street, London, E.C.

The question of corsage is an all-important one, as the fit of a garment depends largely on the shape of the corset. For growing girls, and especially for such as are at all delicate and outgrowing their strength, the Invigorator corset is the least objectionable I have yet seen. That it has the approval of the faculty is in its favour. It may be described as a corset in combination with a chest-expanding brace, and as such corrects the habit of stooping, and by expanding the chest flattens the back and keeps the shoulder-blades in their right place. Speaking as an ex-adjutant, who has had a good deal of experience in "setting-up-drills," it in my opinion possesses for young people merits far superior to anything of the kind yet brought out. It gives support where most wanted without impeding the freedom of the movements of the body; its elasticity is such that respiration and circulation are not interfered with; the chest is thrown out, the back straightened, preserving an erect figure--the body being kept erect by the cross-straps at the back; it is comfortable to the wearer, and there is no undue pressure anywhere. A riding-stay to be perfect should be as light as possible, consistent with due support, boned throughout with real whalebone, so as to be capable of being bent and twisted without fear of "broken busks," and should fit the figure-- not the figure fit it--with glove-like accuracy. Such supple corsets give perfect ease with freedom. The best special maker of riding-corsets for ladies is Madame Festa, 13, Carlos Street, Grosvenor Square, London, W. This artiste's productions combine all that is necessary in material and workmanship, with perfect fit, ease, and grace. A combination of silk elastic and coutil is said to be the ideal material from which really comfortable corsets are made. For winter work they should be lined with a pure natural woollen stuff as soft as a Chuddah shawl. For tropical climates Grass-cloth or Nettle-cloth is strongly recommended.

In this humid, uncertain climate of ours the rider will generally find some sort of light and short waterproof a great comfort. It should be sufficiently long to clear the saddle, and of a material such as will permit of its being rolled up into a small compass for attachment to the Ds of the saddle. Messrs. Lewin and Co., 28, Cockspur Street, S.W. (successors to the old established firm Bax and Co.), makers of the Selby driving-coat, turn out some very neat waterproof tweed or drab garments, which are appropriate and serviceable. Their designs are good, and the material thoroughly to be relied upon.

Well fitting, or in other words, tight gloves, of course, look very well, but horsewomen must preserve free use of their hands. Lightness of hand is an essential, but a certain amount of physical strength cannot be dispensed with, and a tight glove, even of the best quality of kid, means a cramped contraction of the hand and fingers with consequent loss of power. The material, so long as it be stout enough, may be of real buck-skin, dog's-skin, so called, or Cape. The best real buck-skin hunting, driving, and walking-gloves, for either ladies or gentlemen, I have ever come across, are those manufactured by T. P. Lee and Co., 24, Duke Street, Bloomsbury. They are of first-class soft material, well cut, hand-sewn with waxed brown thread, and very durable; in fact, everlasting, and most comfortable wear.

A neat, light hunting-crop, riding-cane, or whip without a tassel, are indispensable.

The following is a comfortable and serviceable riding-dress for long country rides, picnics, etc., recommended by a lady who can boast of considerable experience in the saddle both at home and in the colonies--one of a riding family. "Habit--a short hunting-skirt, short enough to walk in with comfort, with jacket (Norfolk?) of the same material, made loose enough to admit of jersey being worn under it, if required; a wide leather belt for the waist, fastening with a buckle. This belt will be found a great comfort and support when on horseback for many hours. Hat of soft felt, or melon-shaped hat. Pantaloons of chamois leather, buttoning close to the ankles. Hussar or Wellington boots made of Peel leather, with moderate-sized heels, tipped with brass, and soles strong but not thick. A leather stud should be sewn on the left boot, about two and a half inches above the heel, on which stud the spur should rest, and thus be kept in its place without tight buckling. The spur found to be the most useful after a trial of many is a rowel spur of plated steel (the flat tapered-side, elastic, five-pointed hunting), about two to two and a half inches long, strong and light, hunting shape, and fastened with a strap and buckle, the foot-strap of plated steel chain. This chain foot-strap looks neater than a leather one, and does not become cut or worn out when on foot on rough, rocky ground. The rowel pin is a screw-pin; thus the rowel can be changed at pleasure, and a sharp or blunt one fitted as required by the horse one rides." [In lieu of chamois leather I would suggest undressed deer-skin, as supplied by Messrs. E. Tautz and Sons, 485, Oxford Street, London, which is as soft as velvet, and needs no additional lining, so apt to crease. And instead of the boots I recommend waterproofed Russia leather or brown hide, such as men use for polo, as manufactured by Faulkner, 52, South Molton Street, London, W., with low, flat heels tipped with mild steel.] The lady's idea, except with regard to the interchangeable rowel, the pin of which must work loose, is good.

This brings me to the much-vexed subject of the Spur, its use and abuse. Ladies should not be mounted on horses requiring severe punishment; but there are occasions, oft and many, when "a reminder" from a sharp-pointed rowel will prove of service. I do not say that lady riders should always wear a persuader; on a free-going, generous horse it would be out of place, irritating, and annoying; but on a lymphatic slug, or in the case of a display of temper, the armed heel is most necessary. We must bear in mind that almost all of the highest priced ladies' horses have been broken in to carry a lady by professional lady-riders, one and all of whom wear spurs. Many a horse, in the canter especially, will not go up to his bit without an occasional slight prick. Women are by nature supposed to be gentle and kindly, and yet I know some who are everlastingly "rugging" at their horse's mouths and digging in the spur. They would use the whip also as severely as the Latchfords but for the exhibition it would entail. When punishment must be inflicted, the spur as a corrective is far more effective than the whip; it acts instantaneously, without warning, and the horse cannot see it coming and swerve from it. Though more dreaded it inflicts the lesser pain of the two. The deepest dig from the rowel will not leave behind it the smart of the weal from a cutting whip. The best spur for ladies is the one mentioned above, with fine-pointed rowel; it does not tear the habit, and the points are long enough and sharp enough to penetrate through the cloth should it intervene between the heel and the horse's side. No lady should venture to wear a spur till she has acquired firmness of seat, to keep her left leg steady in the stirrup and her heel from constantly niggling the animal's ribs. I do not like the spring-sheath one-point spur, as it is uncertain in its action.

CHAPTER VI.

ALA CAVALIERE.

Much of late has been said and written against and in favour of cross-saddle riding for girls and women. A lady at my elbow has just given her emphatic opinion that it is neither graceful nor modest, and she predicts that the system will never come into vogue or meet the approval of the finer sense of women. The riding-masters are against it to a man, and so are the saddlers, who argue that the change would somewhat militate against their business. We are very conservative in our ideas, and perhaps it is asking too much of women, who have ridden and hunted in a habit on a side-saddle for years, to all at once, or at all, accept and patronize the innovation.

Travellers notice the fact that women never ride sideways, as with us, but astride, like men. It has generally been supposed that the custom now prevailing in Europe and North America dates back only to the Middle Ages. As a fact, the side-saddle was first introduced here by Anne of Luxembourg, Richard II.'s queen, and so far back as 1341, according to Knighton, it had become general among ladies of first rank at tournaments and in public. But the system must have prevailed to some extent in far earlier times, for Rawlinson discovered a picture of two Assyrian women riding sideways on a mule, and on Etruscan vases, older than the founding of Rome, are several representations of women so seated.

There were no horses in Mexico prior to the advent of the Spaniards; indeed, from the progeny of one Andalusian horse and mare, shipped to Paraguay in 1535, were bred those countless mobs which have since spread over the whole southern part of the new Western world, and, passing the Isthmus of Darien or Panama, have wandered into North America. In the great plains of South America, where the inhabitants, all more or less with Spanish blood pulsing through their veins, may be said to live on horseback, it is strange that, without some good cause, the side-saddle should have been discarded for the "Pisana" fashion--the lady riding in front of her cavalier. In Edward I.'s time our fair dames jogged behind their lords, or behind somebody else's lords, in the conventional pillion: then

"This riding double was no crime In the first good Edward's time; No brave man thought himself disgraced By two fair arms around his waist; Nor did the lady blush vermillion Dancing on the lady's pillion."

The attitude of the "Pisana" fashion, though in some cases vastly agreeable, is not highly picturesque, so there must have been some valid reason why the side-saddle, then in general use in Spain, fell out of favour. In long rides, it, as at that time constructed, tired the rider, and caused severe pain in the spine. Nowadays in Mexico and on the Plate River there are magnificent horsewomen who can ride almost anything short of an Australian buckjumper, and who never tire in the saddle, but then they one and all patronize the cross-saddle, riding ala cavaliere or ?la Duchesse de Berri. Their riding garb, and a very becoming one it is, consists of a loose kind of Norfolk jacket or tunic secured at the waist by a belt, loose Turkish pyjamas thrust into riding boots of soft yellow leather, a huge pair of Mexican spurs, and the ladies' "sombrero." Their favourite and, in fact, only pace is a continuous hand-gallop.

Some thirty years ago I remember seeing the ex-Queen of Naples superbly mounted, riding ala cavaliere. Her Majesty was then even more beautiful than her Imperial sister the Empress of Austria, and quite as finished a horsewoman. She wore a high and pointed-crowned felt hat, a long white cloak, something like the Algerian bournouse, patent-leather jack-boots, and gilt spurs. Her seat was perfect, as was her management of her fiery Arab or Barb, the effect charming, and there was nothing to raise the faintest suspicion of a blush on the cheeks of the most modest. There is no doubt that the Duchess de Berri mode of sitting on a horse is much less fatiguing to the rider, gives her more power over the half-broken animals that in foreign countries do duty for ladies' horses, and, in a very great measure, does away with the chance of establishing a raw on the back. In support of the claims of this, to us, novel manner of placing the rider on her horse's back, I quote from Miss Isabella Bird's "Hawaiian Archipelago." Describing her visit to the Anuenue Falls, that lady writes: "The ride was spoiled by my insecure seat in my saddle, and the increased pain in my side which riding produced. Once, in crossing a stream, the horses had to make a sort of downward jump from a rock, and I slipped round my horse's neck; indeed, on the way back I felt that, on the ground of health, I must give up the volcano, as I would never consent to be carried to it, like Lady Franklin, in a litter. When we returned, Mr. Severance suggested that it would be much better for me to follow the Hawaiian fashion, and ride astride, and put his saddle on the horse. It was only my strong desire to see the volcano which made me consent to a mode of riding against which I have a strong prejudice; but the result of the experiment is that I shall visit Kilauea thus or not at all. The native women all ride astride on ordinary occasions in the full sacks, or kolukus, and on gala days in the pan--the gay winged dress which I described in writing from Honolulu. A great many of the foreign ladies in Hawaii have adopted the Mexican saddle also for greater security to themselves and ease to their horses on the steep and perilous bridle-tracks, but they wear full Turkish trousers and jauntily made dresses reaching to the ankles." Writing later from the Colorado district of the Rockies, Miss Bird adds: "I rode sidewise till I was well out of the town, long enough to produce a severe pain in my spine, which was not relieved for some time till after I had changed my position."

Mrs. Power O'Donoghue runs a tilt with all her might against the idea of any of her sex riding like men. But there are so many manly maidens about now who excel in all open-air pastimes requiring pluck, energy, physical activity, and strength, and who attire themselves suitably in a sort of semi-masculine style, that is not asking too much of them to try the virtues of the cross-saddle. Their costumes are not so much neglig?as studiedly, so far as is possible without exactly "wearing the breeches" in public, of the man, manly. One of our Princesses has the credit of being an adept with the foils; our cricket and golf fields are invaded by petticoats of various lengths; we see polo played by ladies on clever blood ponies; they take kindly to billiards and lawn-tennis; and it is whispered of a few that they can put on the "mittens" and take and give punishment. It is not so much the prudery about sitting like men that excites the wrathful indignation of the opponents of cross-saddle riding as the apparent difficulty of deciding upon the thoroughly neat and workwoman-like costume.

The three different costumes represented in these sketches do not differ very greatly in propriety. Shorten No. 3, the Eilitto Muddy-Weather costume--who says there's nothing in a name?--just a trifle and encase the wearer's lower limbs in a pair of Messes E. Tautz and Son's gaiters or leggings, and we have the costume sported the winter before last by a well known lady. It certainly looked, on a wearer of advanced years, a trifle eccentric, but any pretty girl, in her premiere jeunesse, blessed with a good figure and gait, would have been the admired of all admirers. This costume with the funny name is much patronized by lawn-tennis players, golfers, and skaters. Nos. 1 and 2 are as like as "two Dromios," and in no very material degree differ from the short-skirted walking-dress. They have been brought out with an eye to riding ala cavaliere, and being strong and yet neat are intended for prairie-riding in the far West, for the rough-and-ready work of the Australian or New Zealand bush, and for scouring over the veldt of South Africa, or for the hundred and one out-of-the-way places of the earth, whither our English girls venture, from necessity, for adventure, or some more potent attraction. Of the two I prefer No. 1, which is the smarter. It is nothing more or less than a short habit made in the shape of a frock-coat, and is buttoned the whole way down to the knees. The long boots, which, by the way, show off a pretty well-turned ankle and foot to perfection, are certainly a trifle more in evidence than is the case when the lady wears the regular habit and is desirous of showing as little "leg" as possible--a desire, when the foot is threes or narrow fours, and the instep well sprung, not too often indulged. No 2 has a divided skirt.

I do not ask ladies of mature age, or even those whose seat is formed, to don one or other of these costumes, though, after the experience of Miss Bird and others, they might, under similar circumstances, adopt both the costume, and the cross-saddle with advantage. In the backwoods and jungles a wide latitude in dress may be permitted without assailing the strictest modesty.

The fashion of riding in the cross-saddle, if it is to be introduced, as it ought to be, must emanate from the rising generation. The luxury of having both feet in the stirrups, of being able to vary the length of the leather, of having a leg down either side of the horse, and a distribution of the bearing equally on each foot, is surely worthy of consideration when many hours have to be spent in the saddle and long weary distances travelled. If agreeable to the rider, how much more so to the horse? We men know what a relief it is on a long journey to vary the monotonous walk or the wearying trot with an occasioned hard gallop "up in the stirrups," or how it eases one to draw the feet out of the stirrups and let the legs hang free. I have already hazarded the opinion that a lady's seat on a side-saddle is a very firm one, but when she is called upon to ride half-broken horses and to be on their backs for hours at a time, traversing all sorts of country, she undoubtedly is heavily handicapped as compared with a man.

Mrs. O'Donoghue, much to the damage of her own contention, so clearly demonstrates my views that I venture to quote verbatim from one of that lady's published letters. "My companion was in ease while I was in torture. Because he had a leg on either side of his mount, his weight equally distributed, and an equal support upon both sides; in fact he had, as all male riders have, the advantage of a double support in the rise; consequently, at the moment his weight was removed from the saddle, it was thrown upon both sides, and this equal distribution enabled him to accomplish without fatigue that slow rise and fall which is so tiring to a lady whose weight, when she is out of the saddle, is thrown entirely upon one delicate limb, thus inducing her to fall again as soon as possible." As for mere grip--the upright and leaping-heads versus both knees--the security in either case is about the same, but the woman's position in the side-saddle is the more tiring and cramping of the two, and in complete control over the horse, the man's position on the horse has a very decided advantage.

APPENDIX I.

THE TRAINING OF PONIES FOR CHILDREN.

We will take it for granted that the colt, say a three or four year old, is well accustomed to the restraint of the common halter, and is obedient to the cavesson on both sides, also that he leads quietly and bears a fair amount of handling. Were I permitted to explain the Galvayne system, I could, in a very few pages, save the breaker and the colt much time, trouble, and many trials of temper and patience. I have not the professor's permission to make the tempting disclosures. Without trenching on his domain, I may lay down the following rough-and-ready modus operandi, which, however, I am free to confess would be considerably facilitated by a set of his breaking tackle, especially of a particular rope, not made of any vegetable fibre, which, in some cases, exercises a potential control. We must just "gang our ain gait" as my countrymen say.

Having fitted the colt with a soft-lined head-collar-bridle, of the Australian bush pattern, with strong hooks or straps by which to attach the bit, I proceed to bit him. The bit should be on the flexible principle, the mouth-piece being either of chain or a series of ball and socket sections, covered over with white and tasteless rubber, or other soft and yielding material. It should be no thicker than a man's little finger. Inside the cheek and leg of this snaffle I have a large flat disc of sole leather, rounded at the edges, stitched as a guard to prevent the possibility of the bit being drawn through the mouth, of pinching the cheeks against the teeth or in any way injuring the mouth. Every bit, no matter how merciful, will, more or less, make the bars of the mouth tender, but this least of all. If any suffering is evident, or any inflammation set up, then the use of the bit must, till all appearance of undue redness has disappeared, be discontinued. A little tincture of myrrh with eau-de-cologne applied with the fore finger will soon allay the irritation and remove the tenderness.

The best way to insert the bit is, having fixed the near ring to the spring hook or strap on the near side of the head-collar, then coming round to the off side of the head, gentling the pony's head all the time and soothing him, to quietly work the two fore fingers of the left hand into his mouth, and on an opportunity offering, to slip the bit quickly into the mouth. This must be done deftly, without alarming the pony, for if the first attempt result in failure he is certain to throw up his head, run back, and otherwise thwart subsequent endeavours. A little treacle smeared on the bit will make it more palatable and inviting. The first time the bit is in the colt's mouth it should not be allowed to remain more than an hour, and his head must be entirely without restraint. On removing it examine the mouth to see that it has not been injured or bruised, and give him a carrot, or apple. It is immaterial whether these bitting lessons be given in a roomy loose-box, barn, covered-yard, or small paddock.

After becoming reconciled to the bit, strap on a roller or surcingle, having two side and one top ring stitched on to it, the side rings being placed horizontally about where the rider's knees would come, that on the top fore-and-aft. Through these three rings a strong cord should be run forming a sort of running rein, tie the cord to the off-ring of the snaffle, bring it back through the off-side ring, up and through the top ring on the back, down through that on the near side, and so on forward to the near ring of the bit to which it is fastened with a slip knot, taking care that though a slight bearing be upon the bars of the mouth, the colt's head is not tightly reined in and an irksome continuous strain kept on a certain set of muscles of the neck. This running-rein arrangement admits of lateral play of the head, and minimizes the possibility of creating a one-sided mouth.

After a few short lessons in lounging on both sides with his head thus restrained, he may be made to stand in stall with his hindquarters to the manger, the reins being fastened to the post on either side. If the stall, as probably will be the case, be too wide, narrow it by placing sheep hurdles laced with straw on either side of him, so narrowing his standing room that he must preserve a fair "fore and aft" position. The reins must be, if the pillars are too high, fastened to the three rings on the surcingle as explained above. In addition to the single reins there must also be driving reins or cords, carefully adjusted as to length, so as to preserve an even pressure on either side of the mouth, attached to the rings on the manger, so that any attempt to advance is immediately curbed by the strain on the bit.

These lessons should not extend over more than an hour at a time, and during them the trainer should occasionally, by taking the bit in both hands on either side facing him, or by laying hold of the long reins, cause him, exercising only gentle pressure, to rein back, saying at the same time in a tone of quiet command, "back." There will be plenty of room for this in a full-sized stall. He may also be taught to bend his head to the right when the off-rein is pulled upon or even twitched, and so on with the left.

The instructor's aim must be to instil into his mind the firm conviction that it is as impossible to resist the pressure of the bit on either side of the mouth as it is to advance against it. Extreme kindness and gentleness must be exercised in this initial training, each compliance with the teacher's hand and voice being at once met with some encouragement or reward, in shape of a word or two of soothing approval, gentling his head, and a few oats or pieces of carrot or apple--in the tropics sugar-cane or carrot--the bit being removed from the mouth for the purpose. Horses of all sorts are very quick in their likes and dislikes. From the start never let the colt take a dead pull at the reins, let all the pressures be exerted in a light feeling manner with the fingers not the hands.

On becoming fairly proficient at his indoor lesson, we will now, with his Australian bush pattern head-collar-bridle on, a pair of long reins run from the snaffle through the side rings of the surcingle back into the trainer's hands, who will walk behind him, and led by a leading rein attached to the near side of the head-collar but wholly unconnected with the bit, take him into a quiet yard or paddock. He has now to be taught to stop, back, and turn to his bit. The control exercised by the assistant holding the leading rein just suffices to prevent the colt rushing about, or under sudden alarm running back; he will also, though giving him a perfectly free rein, be sufficiently close to his head to aid him in obeying the mandates of the trainor. After walking about as quietly as possible for some time, teaching him how to incline and turn, the feel on the mouth with a moderately tight rein being carefully preserved, he will be on the word "Whoa!" brought to a stand still, and made to stand still and motionless as a well-trained charger on parade.

In the lessons on turning, he may if needful be touched with the whip, only if needful, and then the lash should fall as lightly as the fly from some expert fisherman's rod, the touch of the silk or whip-cord coming simultaneously with the touch on the bars of the mouth. For instance, he is required to turn to the right and hangs a bit on the rein without answering the helm, then a slight touch on the near shoulder will send him up to his bit, give him an inclination to turn smartly in the direction wished for, and the movement may be hastened by the point of the whip being pressed against the off buttock, or upper thigh on the outside. The pull must not be a jerk but a decided lively pull. Always let him go forward as much as space will permit of before making another turn; he must not be confused and so provoked to be stubborn or fight. Let all the turns be to one hand for the first few minutes then turn him in the reverse direction. Should he get his head down and endeavour to establish a steady dead pull, do not indulge him, but step in closer to his quarters so that the strain is at once off the reins, and the moment that he once more feels his bit instantly make him come to a full halt with the word "Whoa." To make a horse stand after being halted, the Arabs throw the bridle over his head and let the rein drag on the ground. When the colt is being broken the bridle is thus left hanging down between his fore legs, and a slave gives it a sharp jerk whenever a step in advance is taken. By this means the horse is duped into the delusion that the pain inflicted on his mouth or nose is caused by his moving while the rein is in this pendant position. What is taught in the desert may be taught in the paddock. The slightest attempt to move forward without the "click" must at once be stopped.

The "backing" lesson is, as a rule, a very simple one, though there are some horses which decline to adopt this retrograde motion. To rein back, the trainer, standing immediately behind the colt, either exerts an even and smart pressure on both reins, drawing them, if need be, through the mouth, when the horse will first bend himself getting his head in handsomely and then begin to step back. At first he will be perhaps, a little awkward, but will soon learn to use his hocks and to adopt this strange gait. If there be any difficulty about getting his head in--it must not be up and out with the bit in the angles of the mouth--the assistant should place the flat of his hand on the animal's face pressing its heel firmly on the cartilage of the nose. The backward movement must cease on the word "Whoa!" and the relaxation of the rein. A horse must not be taught to run back, some acquire the bad habit too readily to a dangerous extent. I may here say that when a horse is given to this vice the best plan is to turn him at once and sharply in the direction he wants to go. In tuition what we want to arrive at is a sort of military "two paces step back, march!"

In these introductory lessons the main use of the assistant with his loose yet ready leading rein is to prevent the colt from turning suddenly round and facing the trainer, a contretemps with a Galvayne's tackle next to impossible. Reins should not, however, be tried at all till the lessons in the loose box and in the stall are so well learnt that there is little or no fear of sudden fright, ebullitions of temper, or other causes of disarrangement and entanglement of the long driving reins. When the habit of yielding to the indication of the rein has once been acquired and well established, it becomes a sort of second nature, which under no circumstances, save those of panic or confirmed bolting, is ever forgotten. A few lessons carefully, firmly, patiently, and completely given will cause the colt to answer the almost imperceptible touch of the rein or the distinct word of command. Once perfected in answering the various signals at the walk, he is then put through precisely the same movements at a trot, and to be an effective teacher, the breaker must not only be a good runner, but in good wind, he must be active enough to show such a horse as "Beau Lyons" at the Hackney Show at Islington. A pony such as is "Norfolk Model," one a hand higher and of a very different stamp, it is true, from what I commend for children, would make a crack "sprinter" put forth his best pace.

During the time the pony is acquiring the A B C or rudiments of his education, he must be frequently and carefully handled. Every effort should be made to gain his confidence. Like all beasts of the field the speediest and surest way to his affection is down his throat; he is imbued with a large share of "cupboard love," so the trainer should always have some tit-bit in his pocket wherewith to reward good behaviour and progress made; moreover, the pupil should be aware of the existence and whereabouts of this store-room. The handling must be general. Rub the head well over with the hands, always working with, and never against the run of the hair. Pull his ears gently (never pull the long hair out from the inside) rub the roots, the eyes and muzzle, work back from the ears down the neck and fore legs, between the fore legs, at the back of the elbows, and along the back, talking to him all the while. Before going to the flanks and hind quarters make him lift both fore feet. If there be any disinclination to obey, a strap should be wound round the fetlock joint, the trainer then taking a firm hold of the ends in his right hand says in a loud voice "Hold up!" at the same time with the palm of the left hand, throwing a portion of his weight on to the near shoulder; this, by throwing the animal's weight over on to the offside, enables the foot to be easily held up.

This lesson imparted, it is extended to the off fore foot. Should the colt, by laying back his ears, showing the whites of his eyes, hugging his tail, and other demonstrations of wickedness, evince his objections to being handled behind the girth, one of the fore feet must be held up and strapped, the buckle of the strap being on the outside of the arm, the foot brought so close to the point of the elbow that no play is left to the knee joint. Then commence to wisp him all over commencing with the head, but, if he is not very restive, do not keep the weight on three legs more than ten minutes at a time, though he, if not overburdened with fat, could easily stand very much longer, or travel a mile or so on three legs. The object, unless vice be displayed, is merely to prevent serious resistance and to convince him that the operation causes no pain. The wisp, the assistant all the time standing at his head speaking in low reassuring tone, patting and caressing him, in the hands of the operator should be at first very gently then briskly applied to the flanks, over the loins, down the quarters and along the channel running between the buttocks, inside the flanks, stifles and haunches, over the sheath, down inside the hocks, in fact anywhere and everywhere known to be tender and "kittle." Having succeeded with the near fore foot up, release it, let him rest awhile and find his way to the store-room dainties. Go through precisely the same lesson with the right foot up, on this occasion giving special attention to those parts which he most strongly objects to being handled. Dwell over his hocks and the inside of his stifles, handle his tail, freely sponging his dock out, running the sponge down through the channel over the sheath, the inside of the thighs and hocks. Release the fore foot, and if he will stand a repetition of all these liberties quietly, he has learnt one important part of his education.

Elsewhere I have endeavoured to describe the unsophisticated antics displayed by the fresh-caught Australian buck-jumper and the inveterate plunger in endeavouring to dislocate their riders. In the one case it is the untaught, unpractised effort of an animal in a paroxysm of fear; in the other the vice of the artful, tricky, practitioner. In either case the horseman may be, very often is, "slung" handsomely, wondering, as he picks himself up, dazed and bewildered with an incoherent idea as to what had befallen him, and how he got there. If a wild horse suddenly finds a panther or a tiger on his back, he at once, in terror, endeavours by a succession of flings to get rid of the incubus. So it is with the unbroken colt bred in captivity, and especially so with the pony fresh from his native hills or pastures. What must be his astonishment when, for the first time he feels a saddle tightly girthed to his back, and the weight of some one in it? His first and only feeling is that of fear, so, being prevented by the bit and bridle from rushing off at the verge of his speed, he by bucks, plunges, and kicks, sets to work to throw the rider.

In mounting the colt the first attempts at making him quite quiet during the process should be in the direction of eliminating every sense of fear. As saddles, especially if badly stuffed and cold, are the cause of many back troubles, I prefer to have him, in the first instance, ridden in a rug or sheepskin, the wool next his hair, kept in its place by a broad web surcingle. Hold the rug or skin to his nose, and let him smell and feel it, rub it over his head, down his neck, in fact all over him, not neatly folded up but loose; toss it about, drag it over him, round him, between his fore legs, under his belly, and out between his thighs. When he takes no heed of it, fold it up on his back and girth it on with the surcingle. Then lead him out for half an hour or so occasionally, pulling up to lean a good bit of weight on his back.

On returning to the loose box, covered yard, or paddock, the first lesson in mounting will be commenced. Having secured the services of some active smart lad who can ride and vault, the lighter the better, make him stand on a mounting block, an inverted empty wine chest will do, placed near his fore leg. If the pony be nervous at this block, let him examine it, smell it, touch it, and even eat a few carrots off it. Standing on this coign of advantage, the lad must loll over him, patting him, reaching down well on the off side, leaning at first a portion, and then his whole weight on him. If he makes no objection to this treatment, the lad should seat himself on his back, mounting and dismounting repeatedly, slowly but neatly, being careful not to descend on his back with a jerk. So long as the colt shows no fear, this gymnastic practice may be varied with advantage to almost any extent, the contact of the gymnast's body with that of the pony being as close as possible. He should not only vault all over him and straddle him, but should crawl and creep all over him and under him, winding up by vaulting on his back, over his head, and over his quarters. I have frequently taught Arabs to put their heads between my legs and by the sudden throw-up of their necks to send me into the saddle face to the tail. On no account hurry this mounting practice, do not let him be flustered or fatigued, and see that the rider's foot deftly clears him without once touching or kicking him; much depends on the clean manner in which the various mountings and dismountings are performed.

The mounting block will be dispensed with so soon as the rider is permitted to throw his right leg over his back and to straddle him without starting. It is essential that he should stand stock still and that he should not move forward without the usual "klick." When quite patient and steady in being mounted with the rug or fleece, a nice light 5 lb. polo or racing saddle with a "Humane" numnah under it should be substituted, and if the pony's shoulders are low and upright a crupper will be necessary. Care must be taken that the crupper strap is not too tight, also that the crupper itself does not produce a scald under the dock of the tail; a strip of lamb-skin, the wool next the dock, will ensure that. After being led about in the saddle for a time, he is brought into the box or yard and there mounted by the lad, the trainer having hold of the leading rein, the rider of the bridle.

Now a word as to the said lad. All he has to do is to preserve the lightest possible touch of the mouth, and to sit firm and sit quiet. I would rather prefer that he did not hail from a racing stable, for these imps--the most mischievous of their race--are up to all sorts of tricks and are accustomed to ride trusting almost entirely to the support gained from their knotted bridle and the steady pressure against the stirrup somewhat after the principle of the coachman and his foot-board. He must be forced to keep his heels and his ashplant quiet. I am averse to much lounging and am confident it is overdone. On carrying the lad quietly led by hand, the following lessons should be in company with some staid old stager. Markedly gregarious in his habits, the horse never feels so happy or contended as when in company; in the society of a well-behaved tractable member of his family he will do all that is required of him. Soon the leading rein will be superfluous and the pony and his rider will be able to go anywhere at any pace. It is especially advisable that when his first rides lie away from home he should be ridden in company with some other horse, or he may turn restive. Be very careful not to attempt anything with him that may lead up to a fight in which he may remain master. Any disposition on his part to "reest" or to break out into rebellion is proof of his not having learnt his first lessons properly. Far better to lead him away from home for a mile or two and then to mount him, than to hazard any difference of opinion. The example of a well-broken, well-ridden, well-mannered horse is very important. One act of successful disobedience may undo the careful labour of weeks and necessitate very stringent measures, such as those described in my previous volume, in the case of confirmed vice.

Weeks of careful riding always under the trainer's eye, will be required before the lessons are complete, and the pupil sobered down so as to be a safe and comfortable conveyance for children beginners.

Printed in Great Britain
by Amazon

41484409R00036